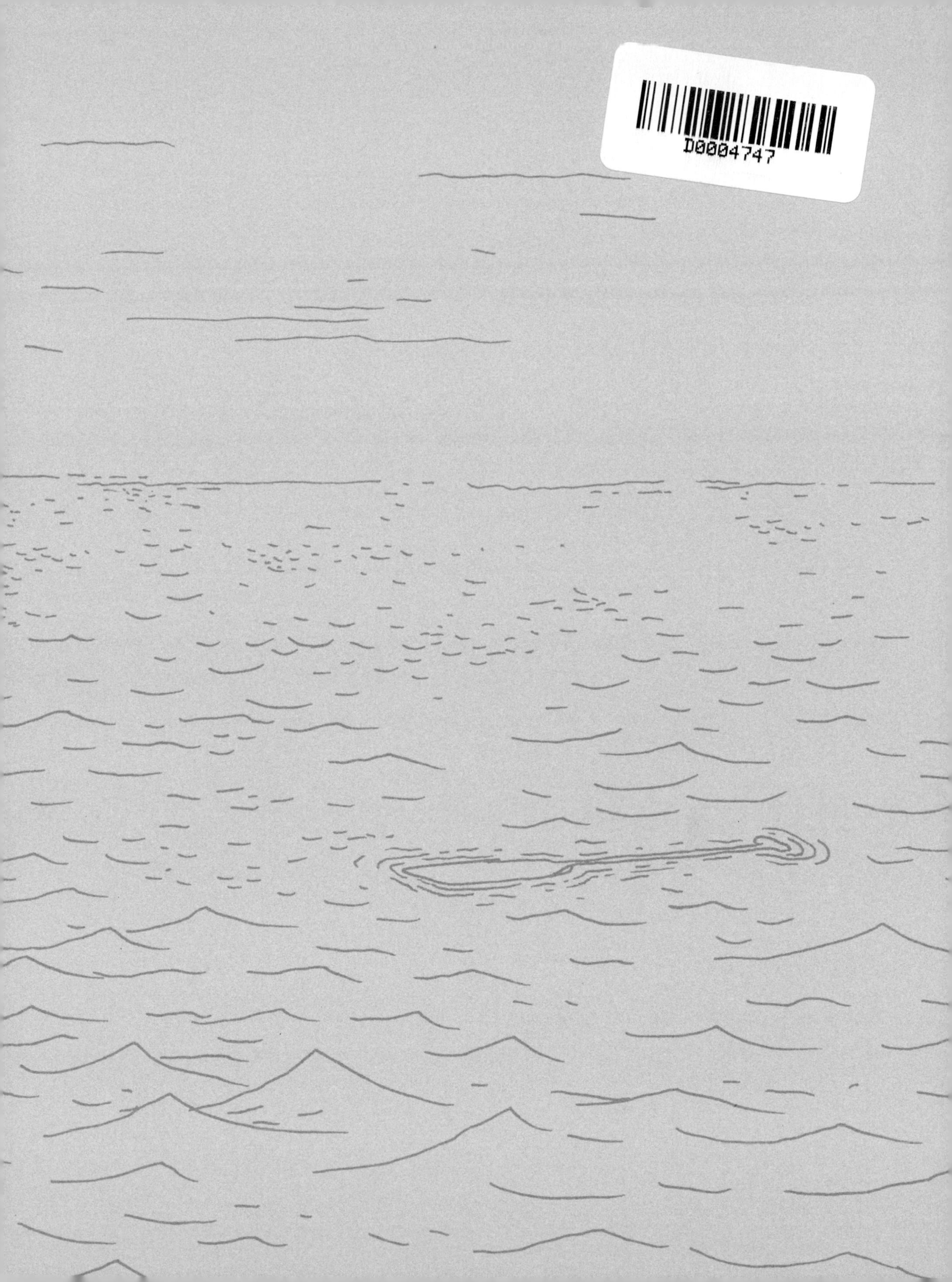

Thanks to Chris Oliveros, Sammy Harkham,
David Heatley, Paul Hornschemeier, Kevin Huizenga,
Ulla Nilsen, Solveig Nilsen, and Cheryl Weaver.
This book is dedicated to Cheryl Weaver with love
and thanks. It was a nice walk.

Correspondence: ndrs@hotmail.com
also: www.theholyconsumption.com

Drawn & Quarterly
Post Office Box 48056
Montreal, Quebec
Canada H2V 4S8
www.drawnandquarterly.com

First hardcover edition: May 2007.
10 9 8 7 6 5 4 3 2 1
Printed in Singapore.

Library and Archives Canada Cataloguing in Publication
Nilsen, Anders, 1973-
Dogs and water / Anders Nilsen.
ISBN 978-1-897299-08-1 I. Title. PN6727.N56D64 2007   741.5973   C2006-905532-7

Distributed in the USA by:
Farrar, Straus and Giroux
19 Union Square West
New York, NY 10003
Orders: 888-330-8477

Distributed in Canada by:
Raincoast Books
9050 Shaughnessy Street
Vancouver, BC V6P 6E5
Orders: 800-663-5714

Distributed in the United Kingdom by:
Publishers Group U.K.
8 The Arena
Mollison Avenue
Enfield Middlesex EN3 7NL
Orders: 0208-8040400

DOGS and WATER

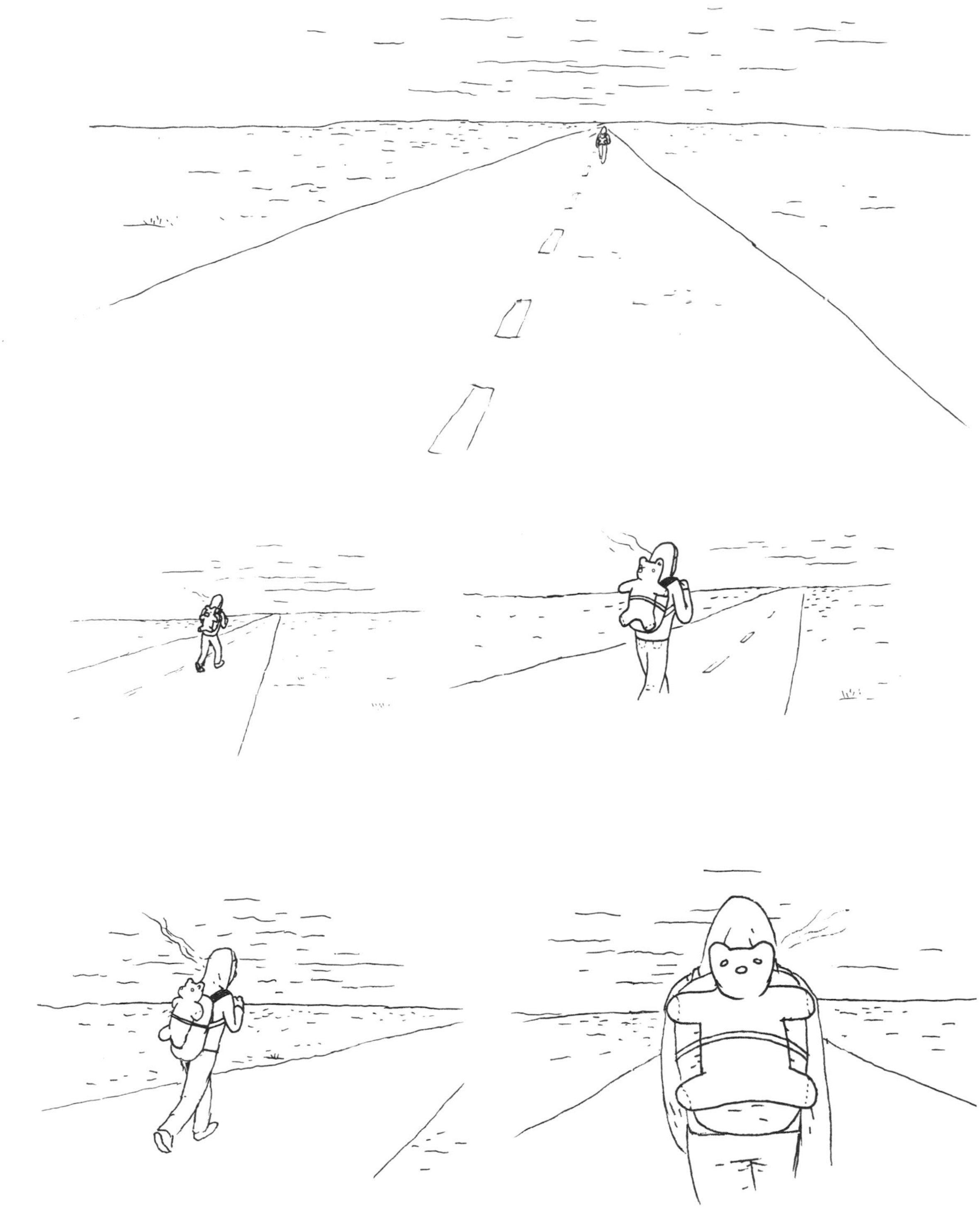

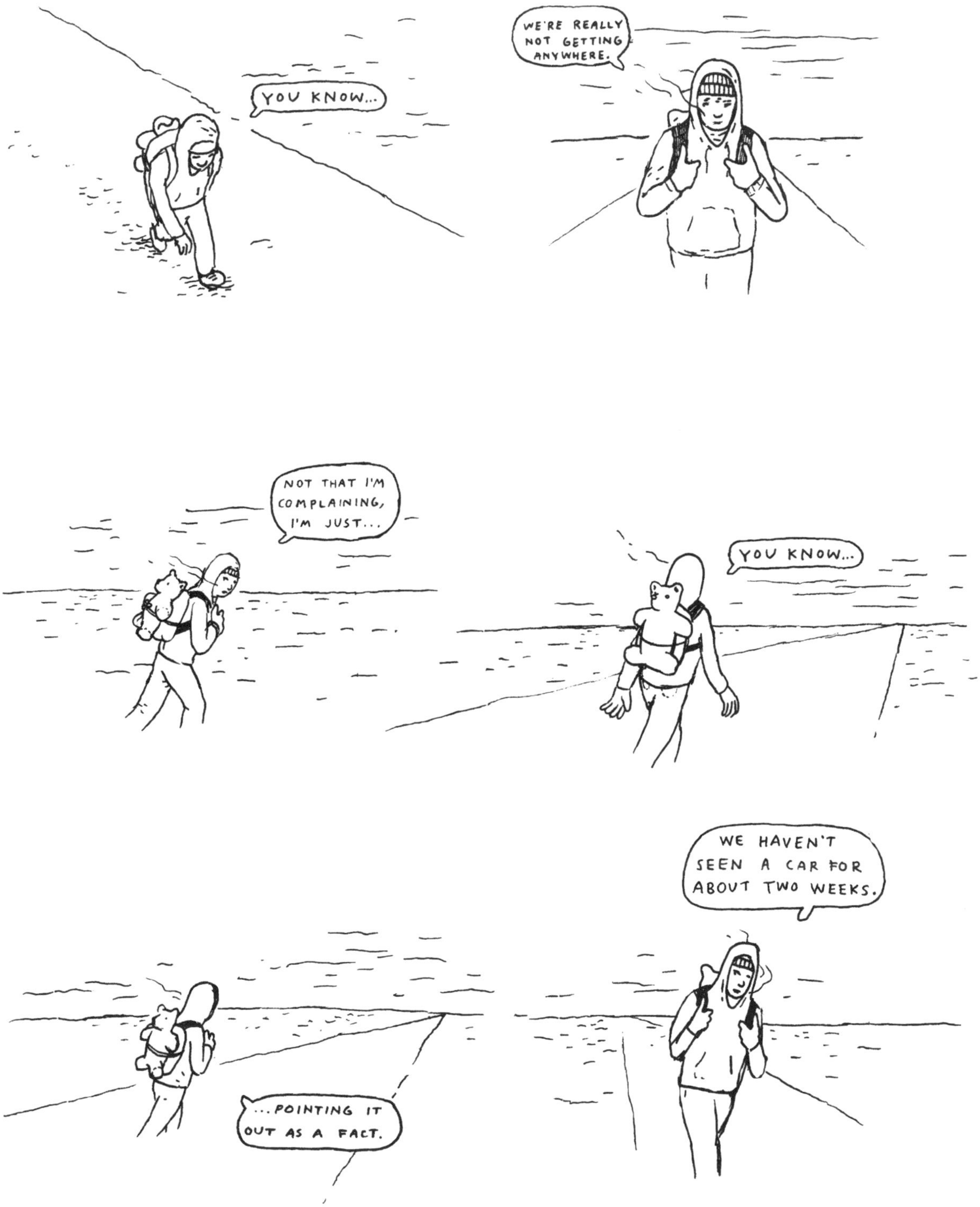
YOU KNOW...
WE'RE REALLY NOT GETTING ANYWHERE.
NOT THAT I'M COMPLAINING, I'M JUST...
YOU KNOW...
...POINTING IT OUT AS A FACT.
WE HAVEN'T SEEN A CAR FOR ABOUT TWO WEEKS.

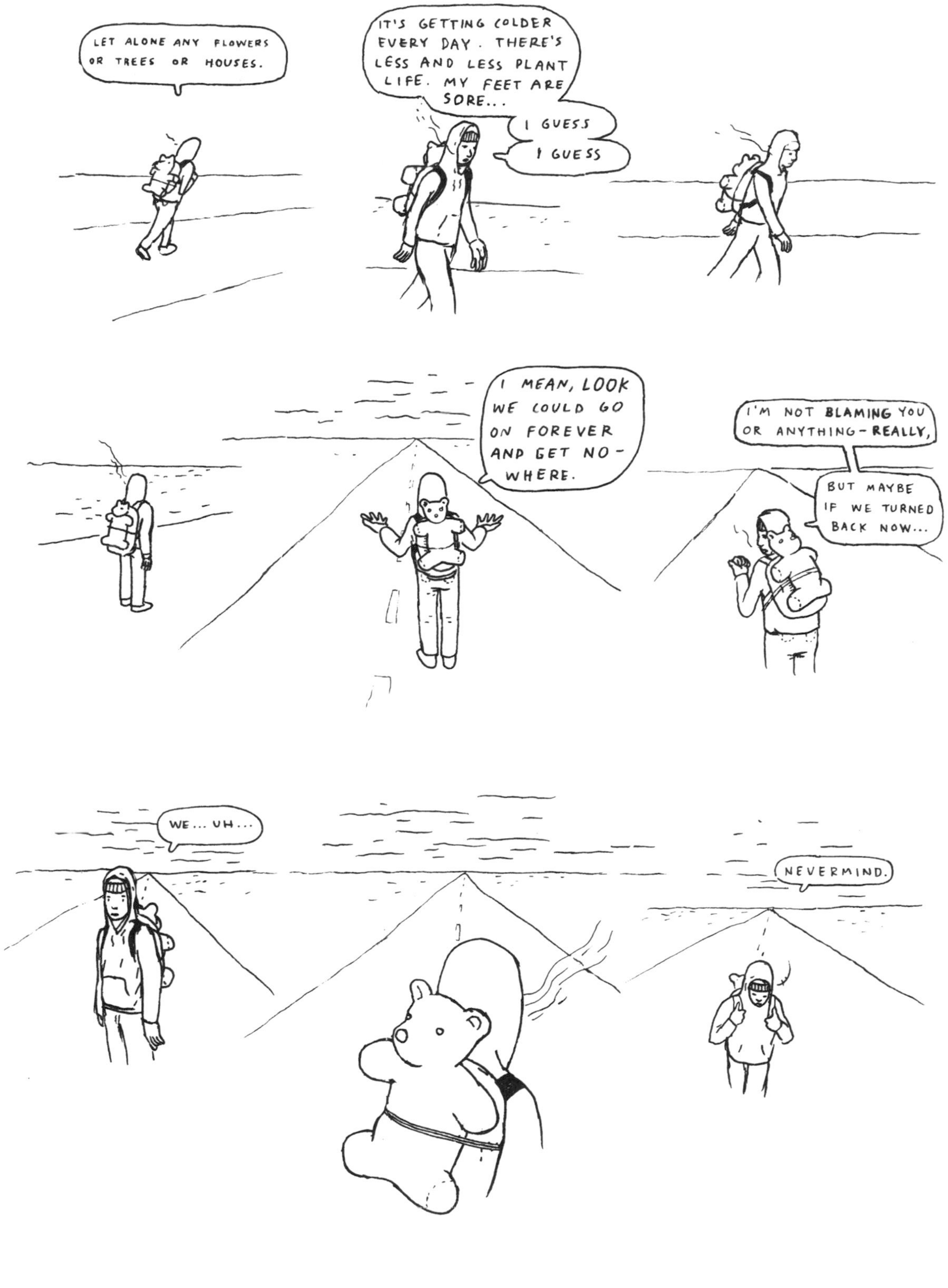
LET ALONE ANY FLOWERS OR TREES OR HOUSES.
IT'S GETTING COLDER EVERY DAY. THERE'S LESS AND LESS PLANT LIFE. MY FEET ARE SORE...
I GUESS
I GUESS
I MEAN, LOOK WE COULD GO ON FOREVER AND GET NO-WHERE.
I'M NOT BLAMING YOU OR ANYTHING-REALLY,
BUT MAYBE IF WE TURNED BACK NOW...
WE... UH...
NEVERMIND.

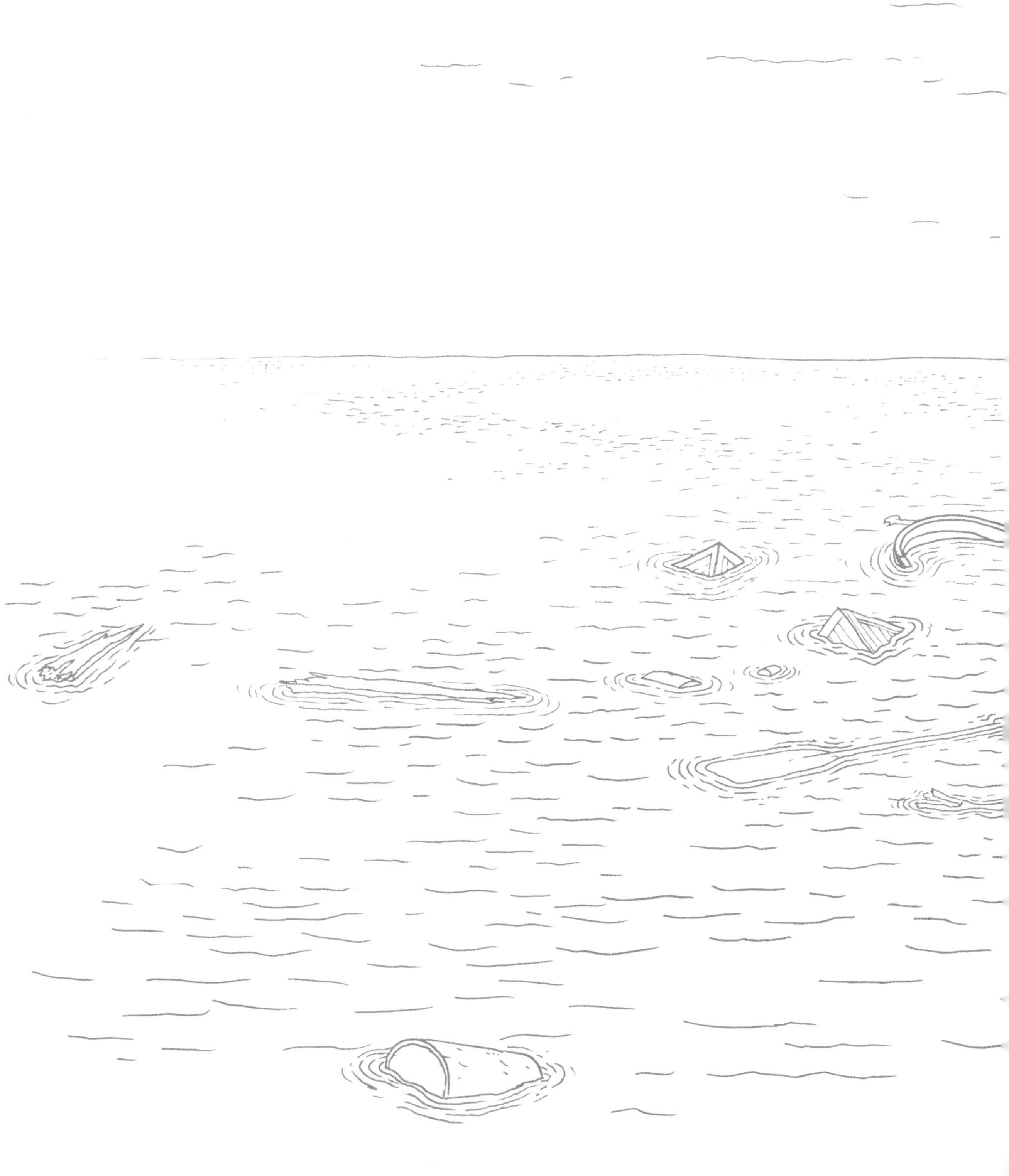

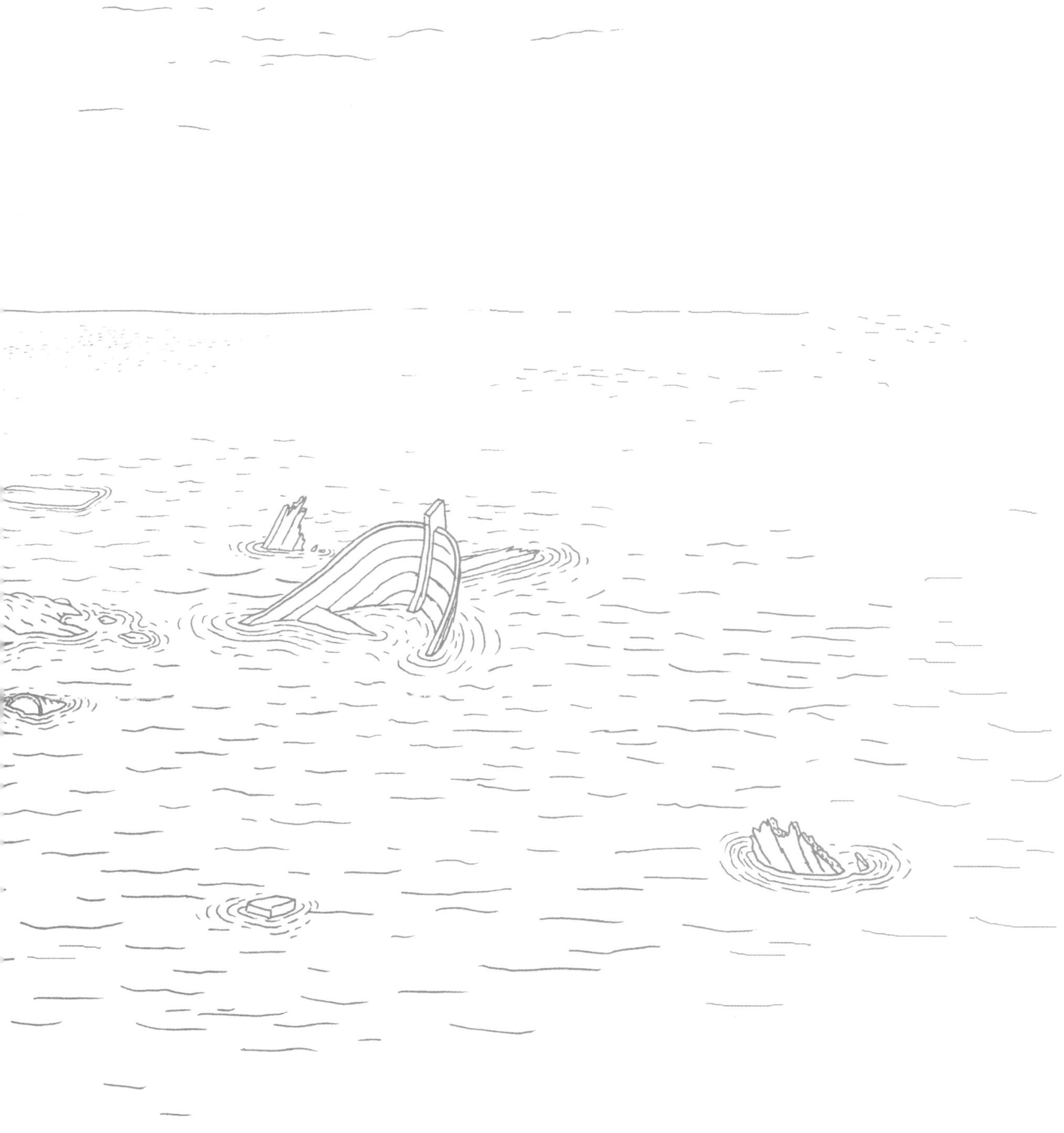

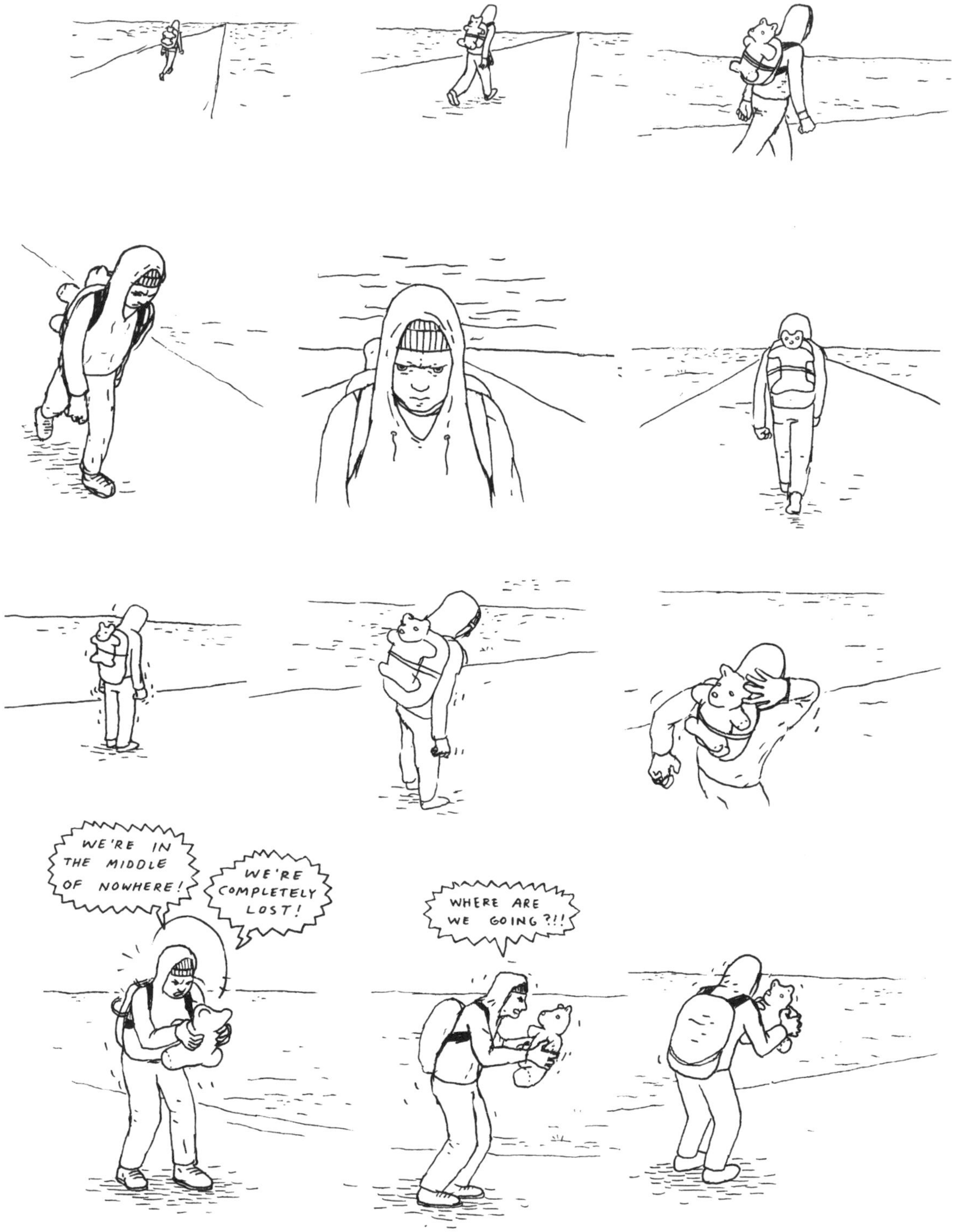
WE'RE IN THE MIDDLE OF NOWHERE!
WE'RE COMPLETELY LOST!
WHERE ARE WE GOING?!!

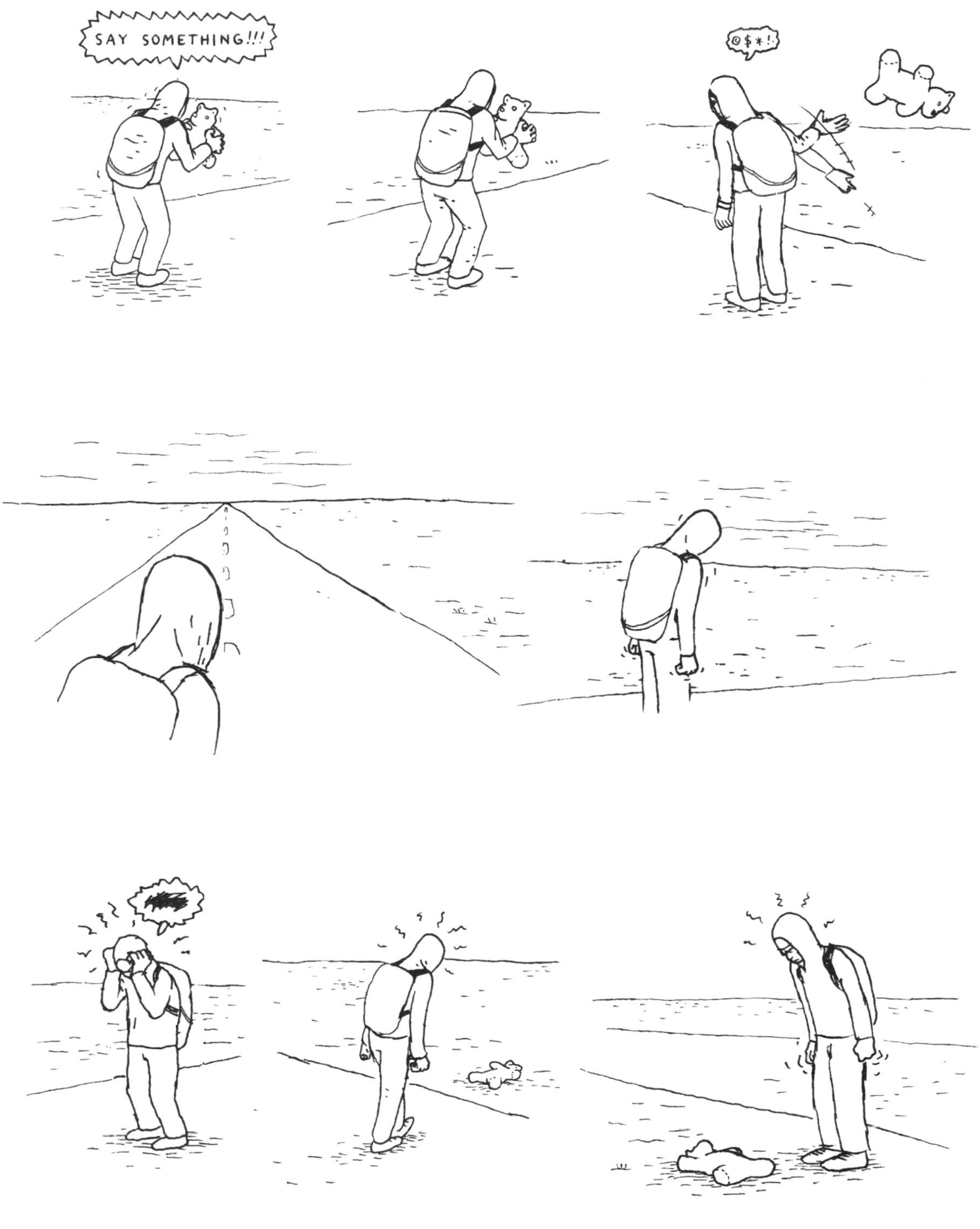
SAY SOMETHING!!!
@$*!

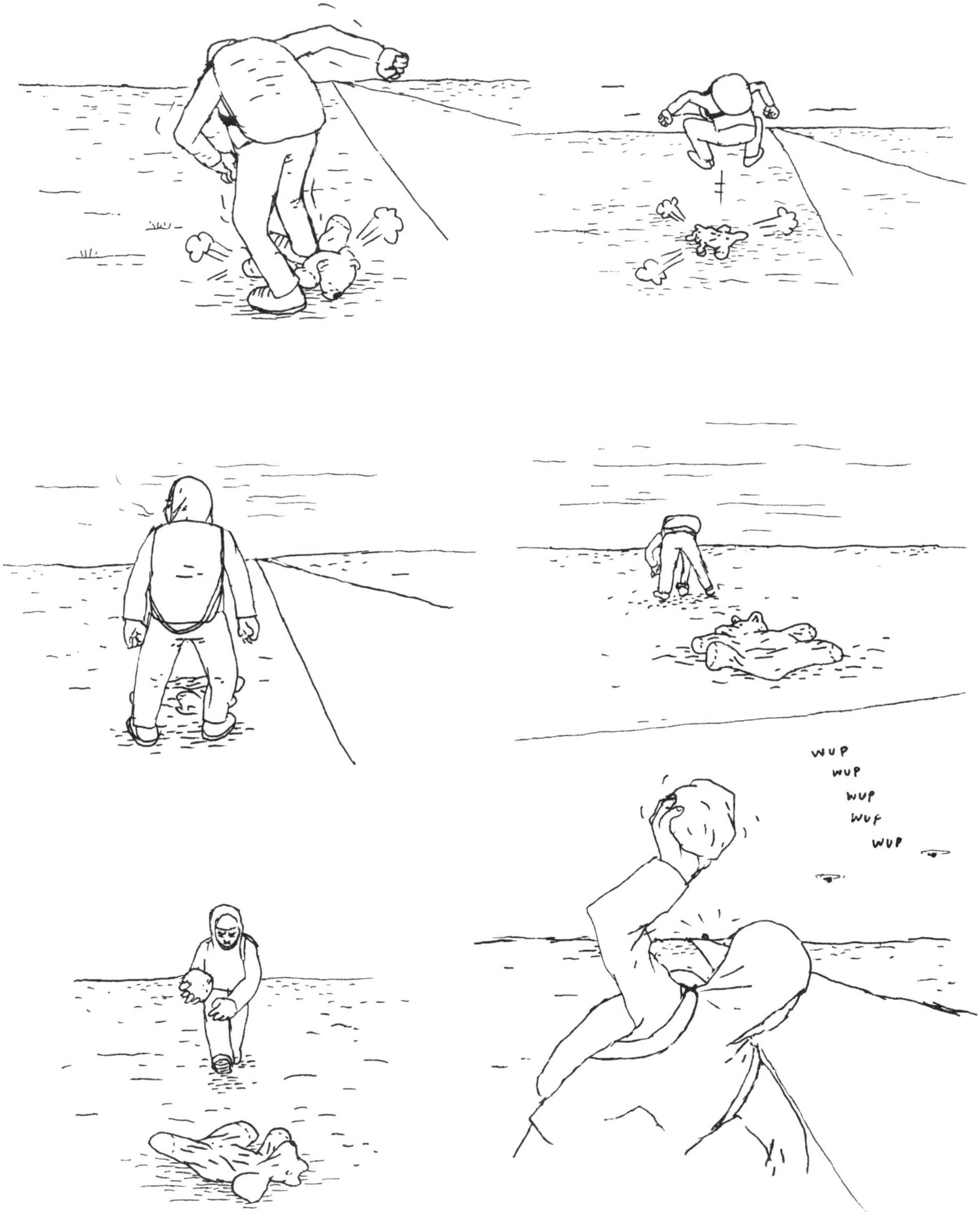
WUP
WUP
WUP
WUP
WUP

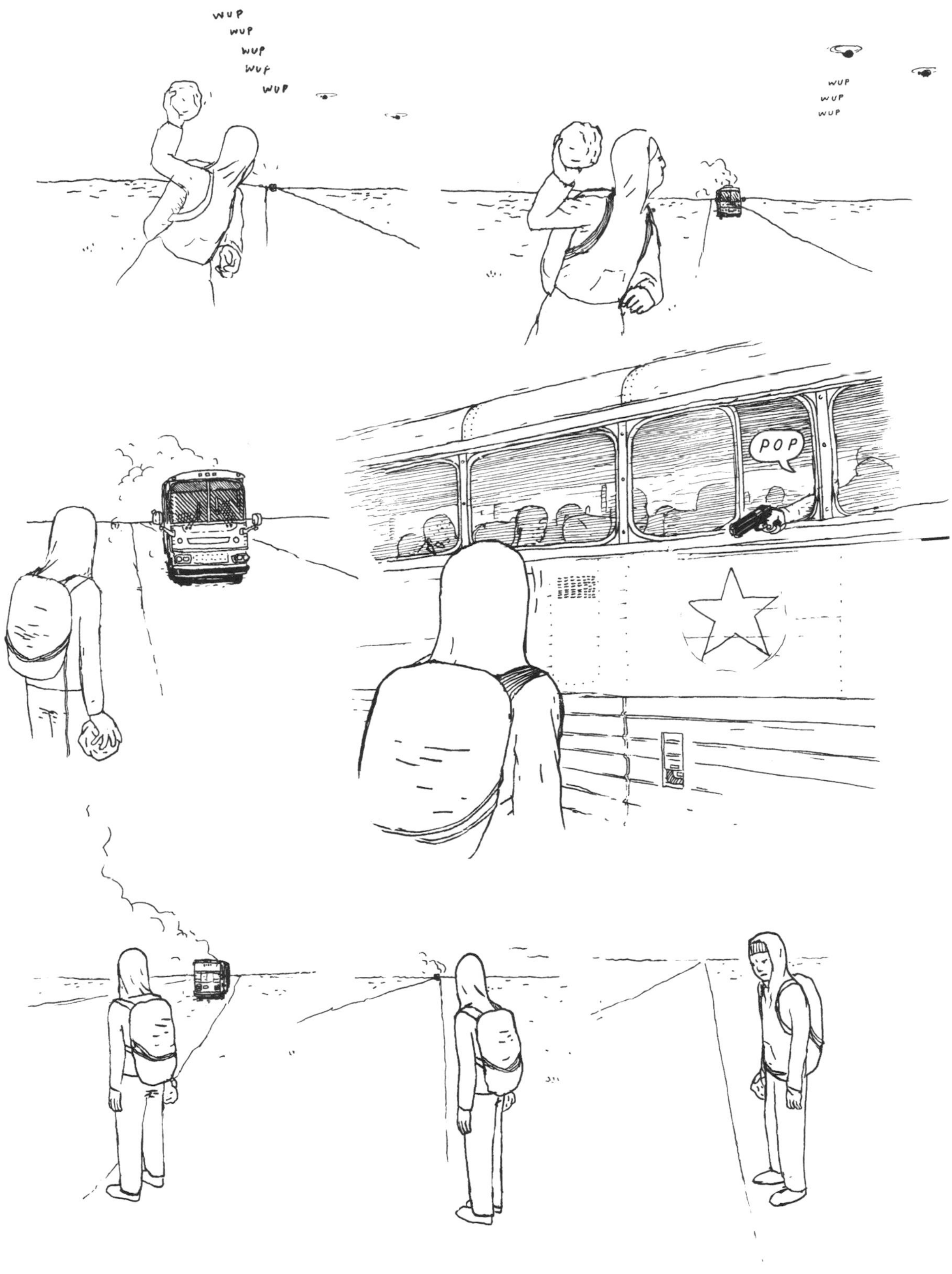
WUP
WUP
WUP
WUF
WUP
WUP
WUP
WUP
POP

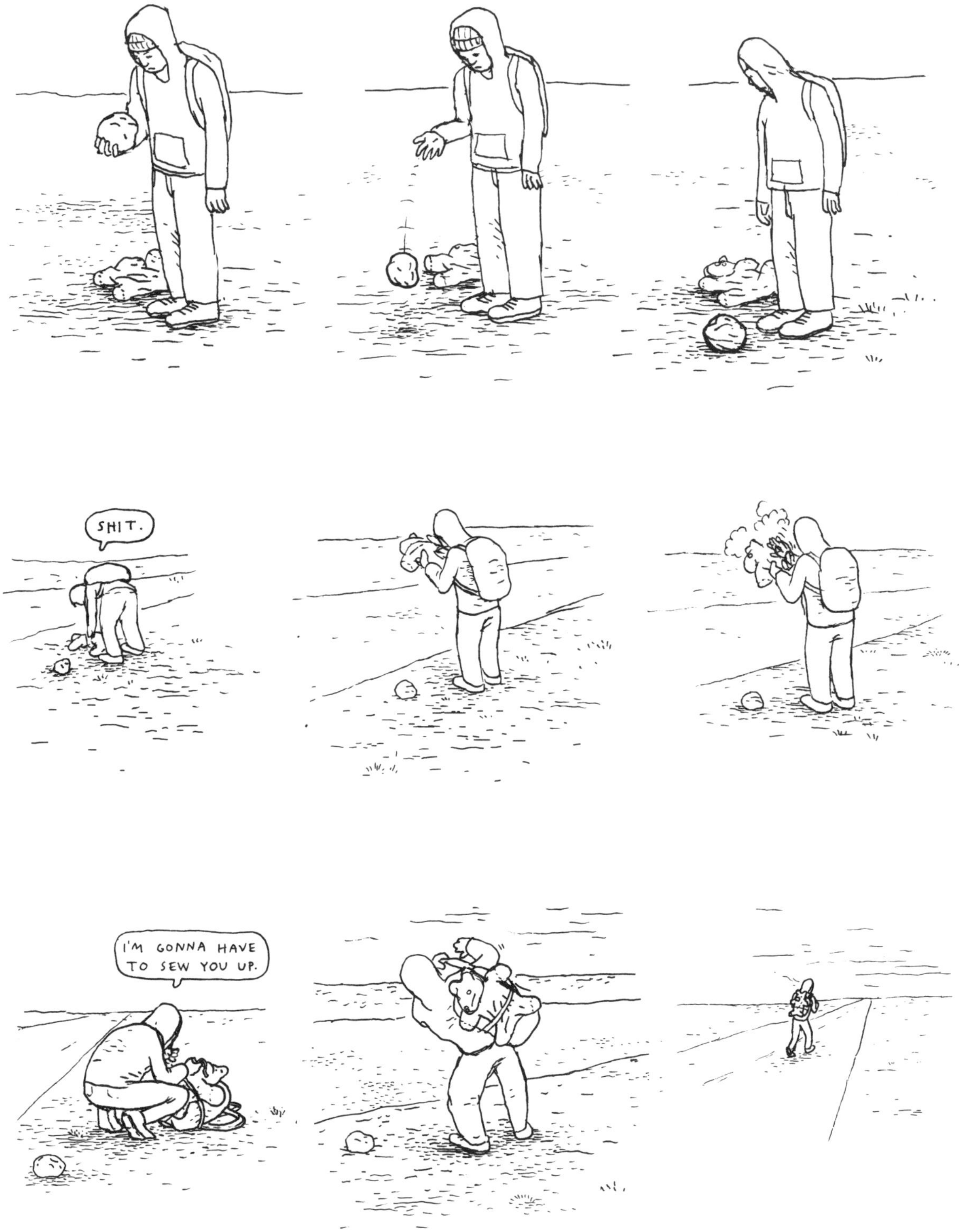
SHIT.
I'M GONNA HAVE TO SEW YOU UP.

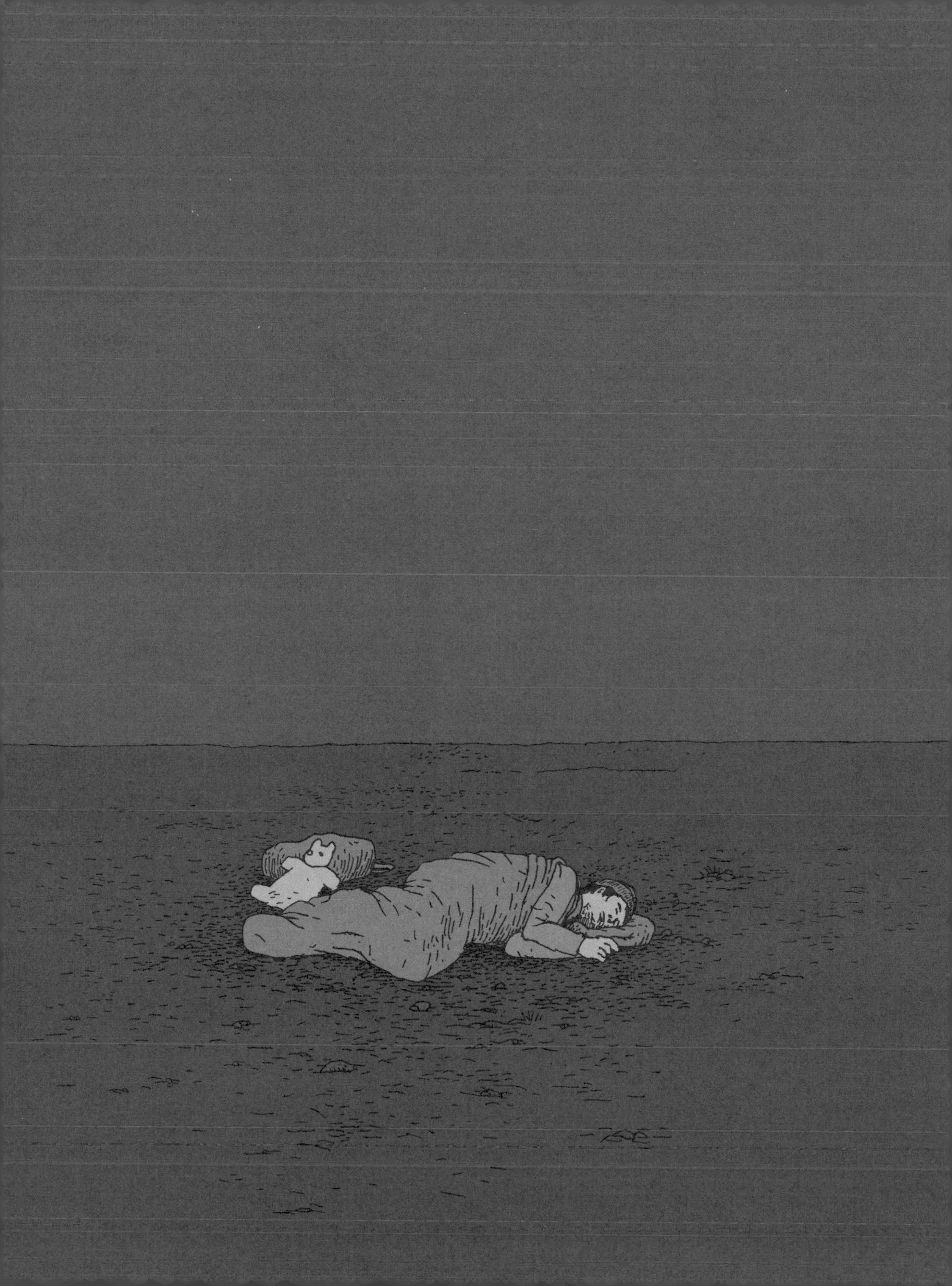

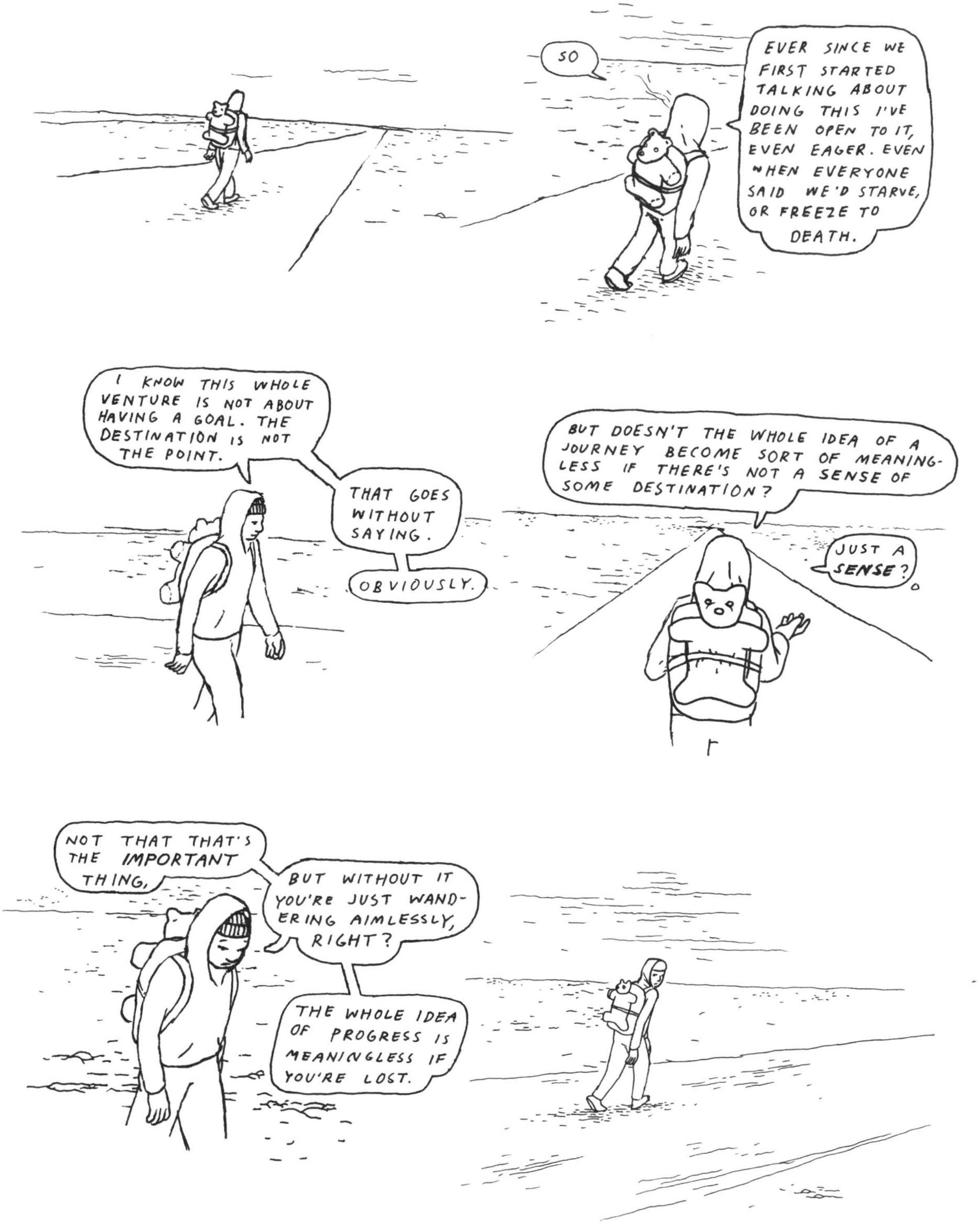
SO
EVER SINCE WE FIRST STARTED TALKING ABOUT DOING THIS I'VE BEEN OPEN TO IT, EVEN EAGER. EVEN WHEN EVERYONE SAID WE'D STARVE, OR FREEZE TO DEATH.
I KNOW THIS WHOLE VENTURE IS NOT ABOUT HAVING A GOAL. THE DESTINATION IS NOT THE POINT.
THAT GOES WITHOUT SAYING.
OBVIOUSLY.
BUT DOESN'T THE WHOLE IDEA OF A JOURNEY BECOME SORT OF MEANINGLESS IF THERE'S NOT A SENSE OF SOME DESTINATION?
JUST A SENSE?
NOT THAT THAT'S THE IMPORTANT THING,
BUT WITHOUT IT YOU'RE JUST WANDERING AIMLESSLY, RIGHT?
THE WHOLE IDEA OF PROGRESS IS MEANINGLESS IF YOU'RE LOST.

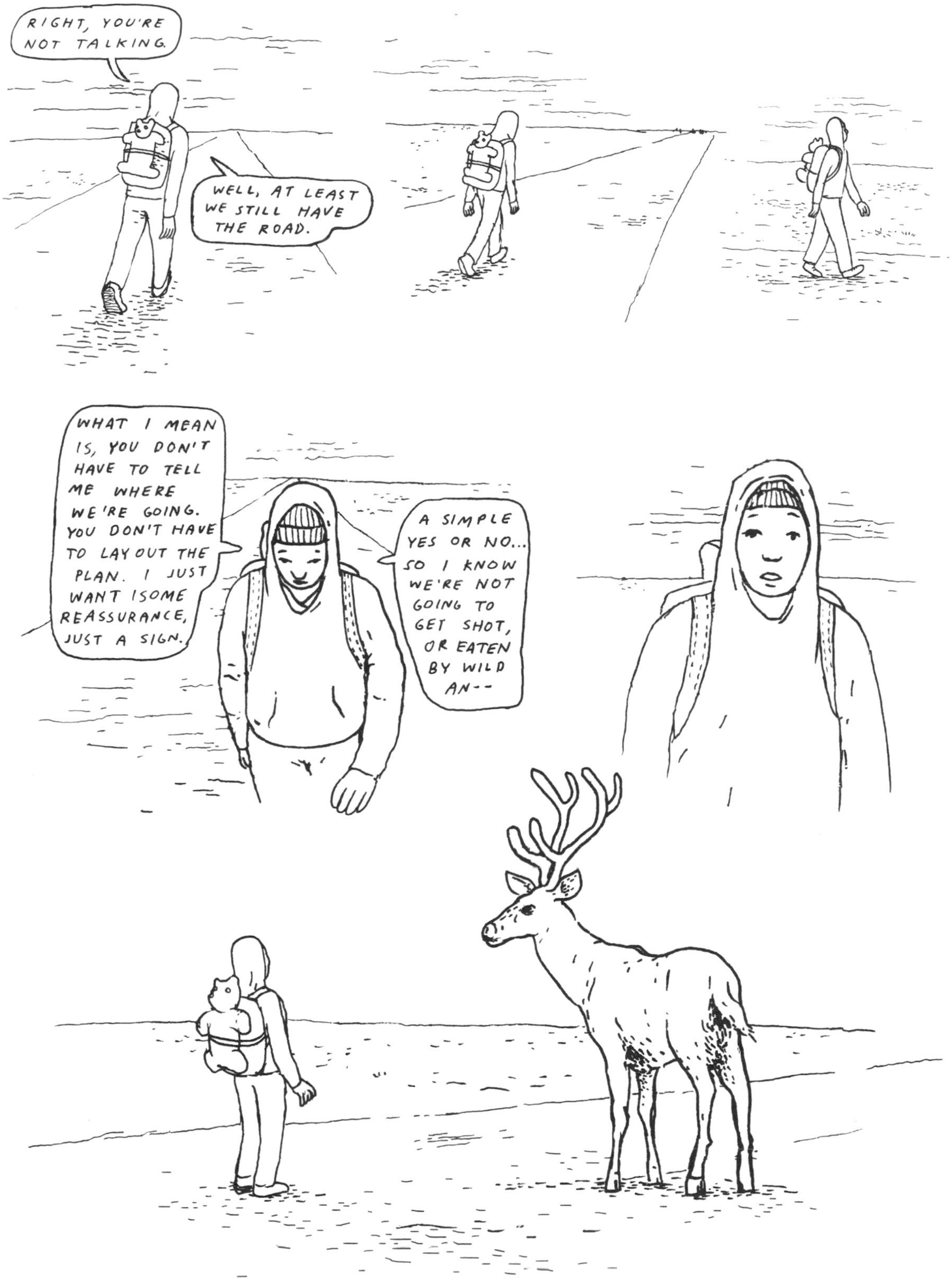
RIGHT, YOU'RE NOT TALKING.
WELL, AT LEAST WE STILL HAVE THE ROAD.
WHAT I MEAN IS, YOU DON'T HAVE TO TELL ME WHERE WE'RE GOING. YOU DON'T HAVE TO LAY OUT THE PLAN. I JUST WANT ISOME REASSURANCE, JUST A SIGN.
A SIMPLE YES OR NO... SO I KNOW WE'RE NOT GOING TO GET SHOT, OR EATEN BY WILD AN--

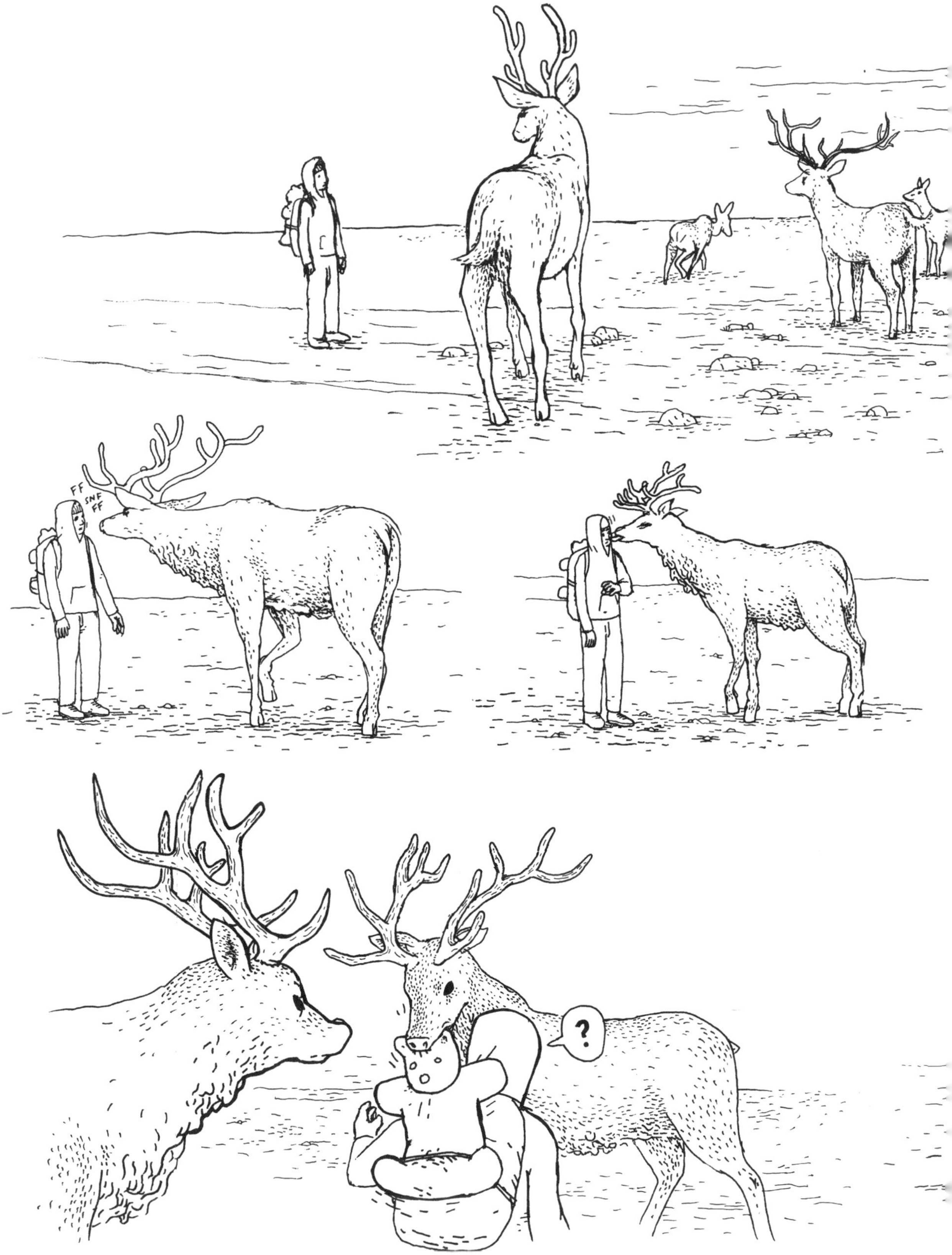
FF
SNF
FF
?

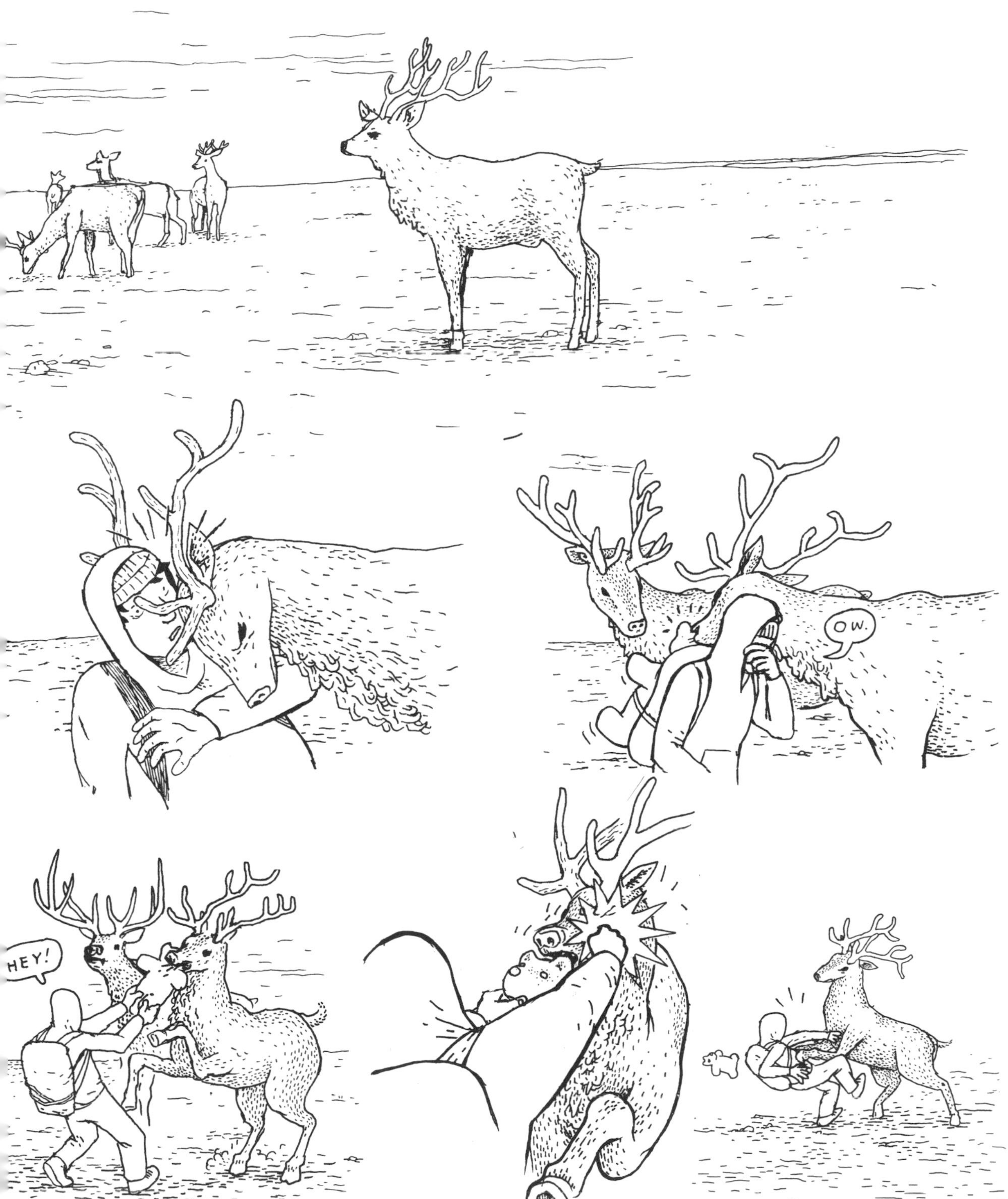
OW.
HEY!

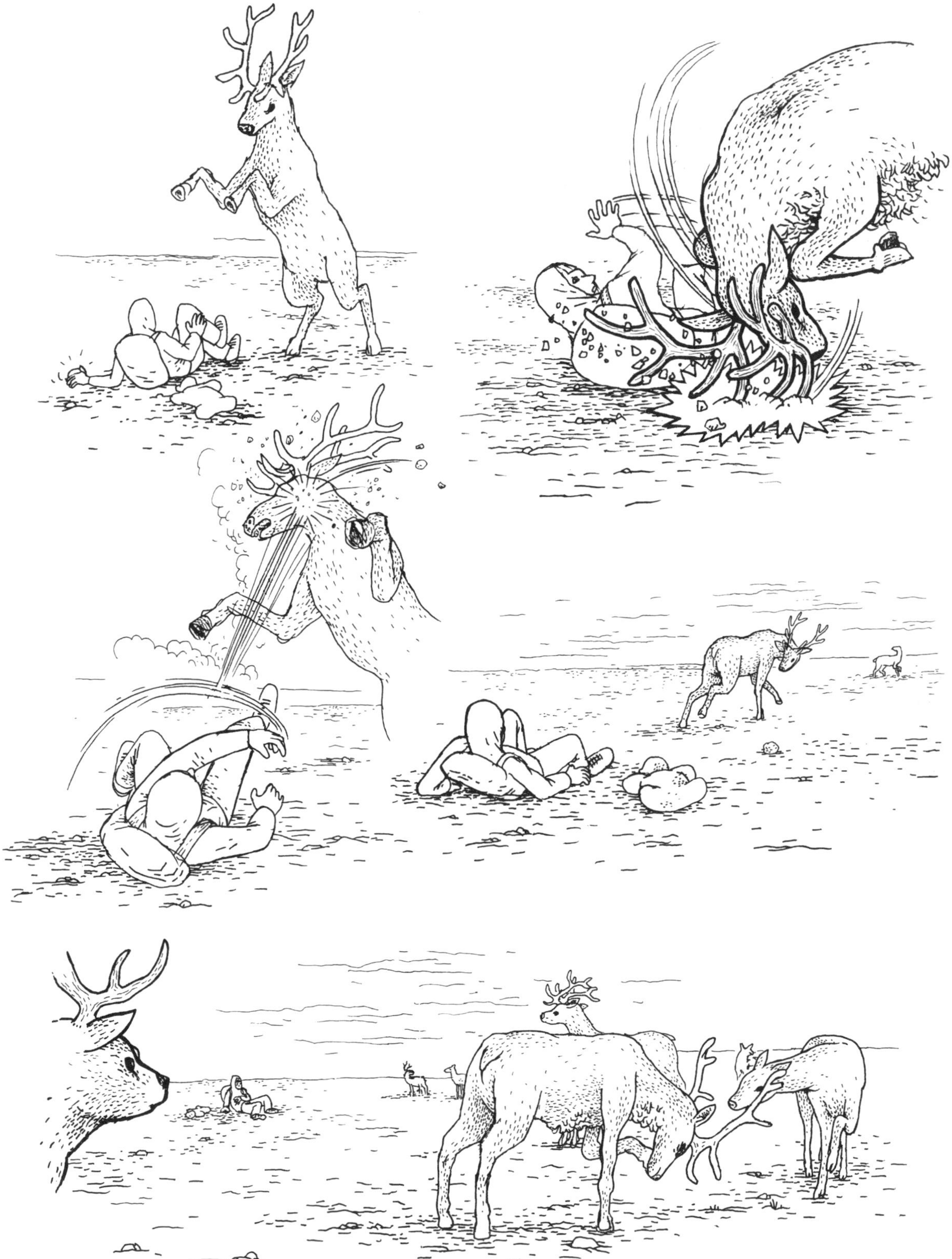

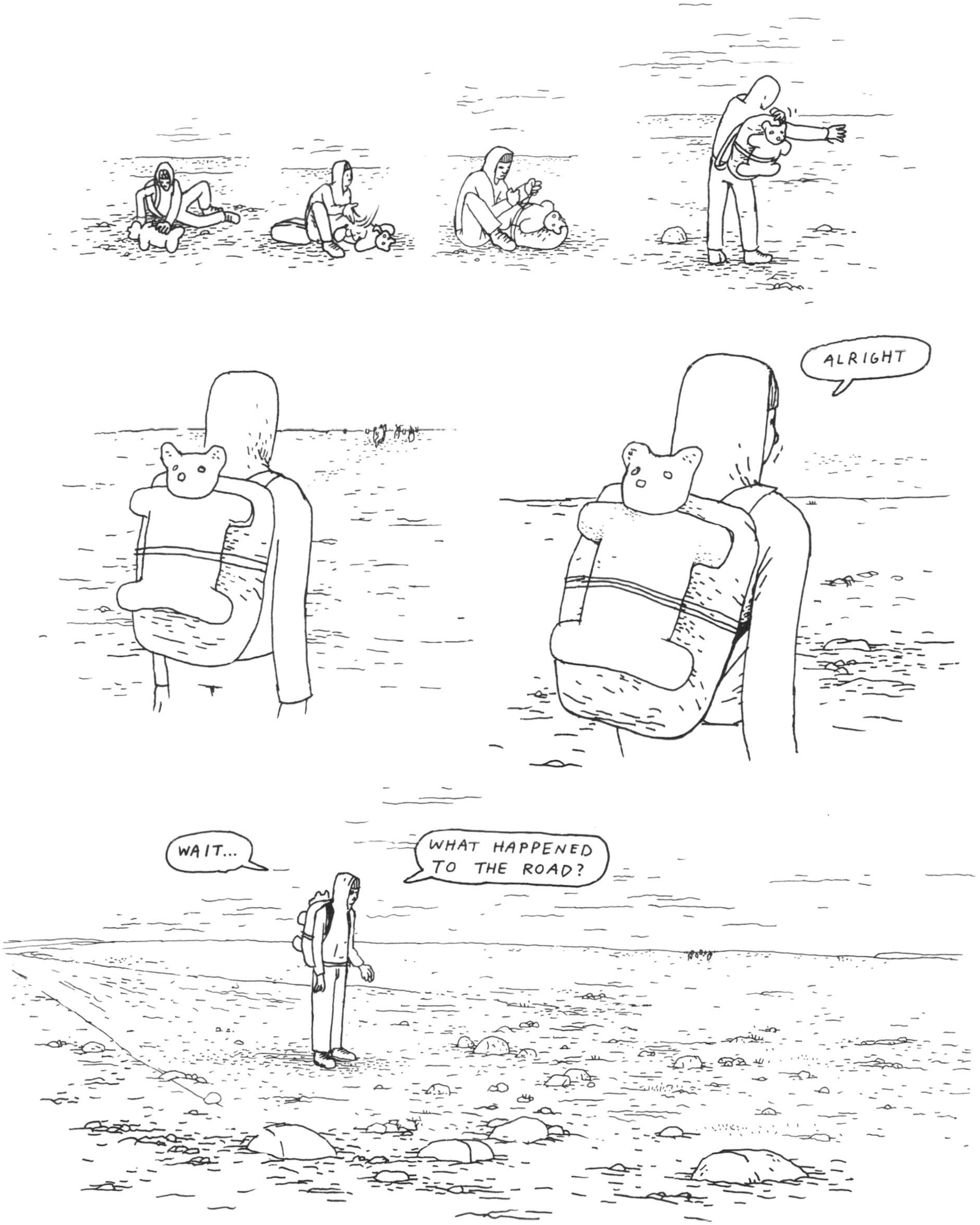
ALRIGHT
WAIT...
WHAT HAPPENED TO THE ROAD?

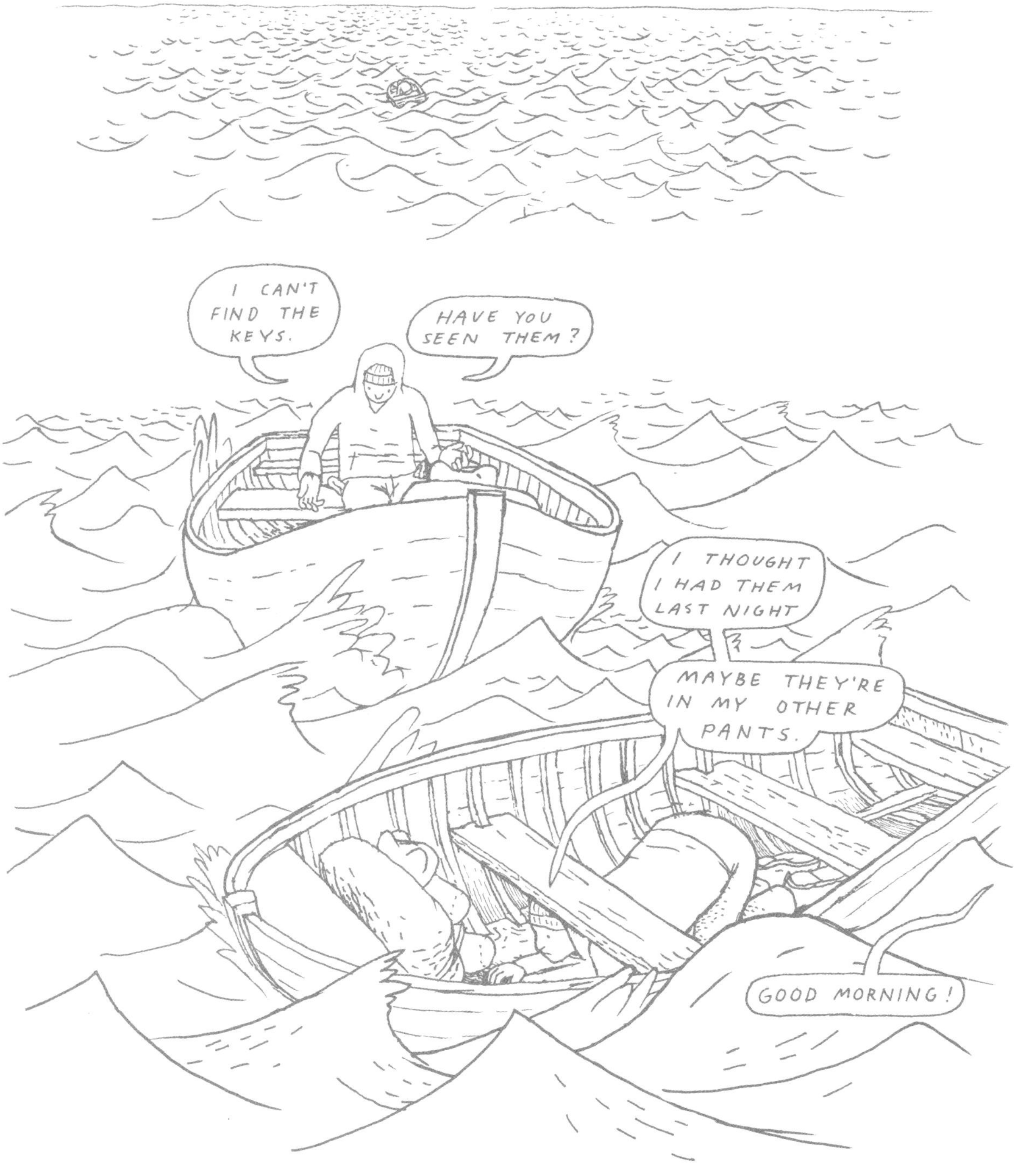
I CAN'T FIND THE KEYS.
HAVE YOU SEEN THEM?
I THOUGHT I HAD THEM LAST NIGHT
MAYBE THEY'RE IN MY OTHER PANTS.
GOOD MORNING!

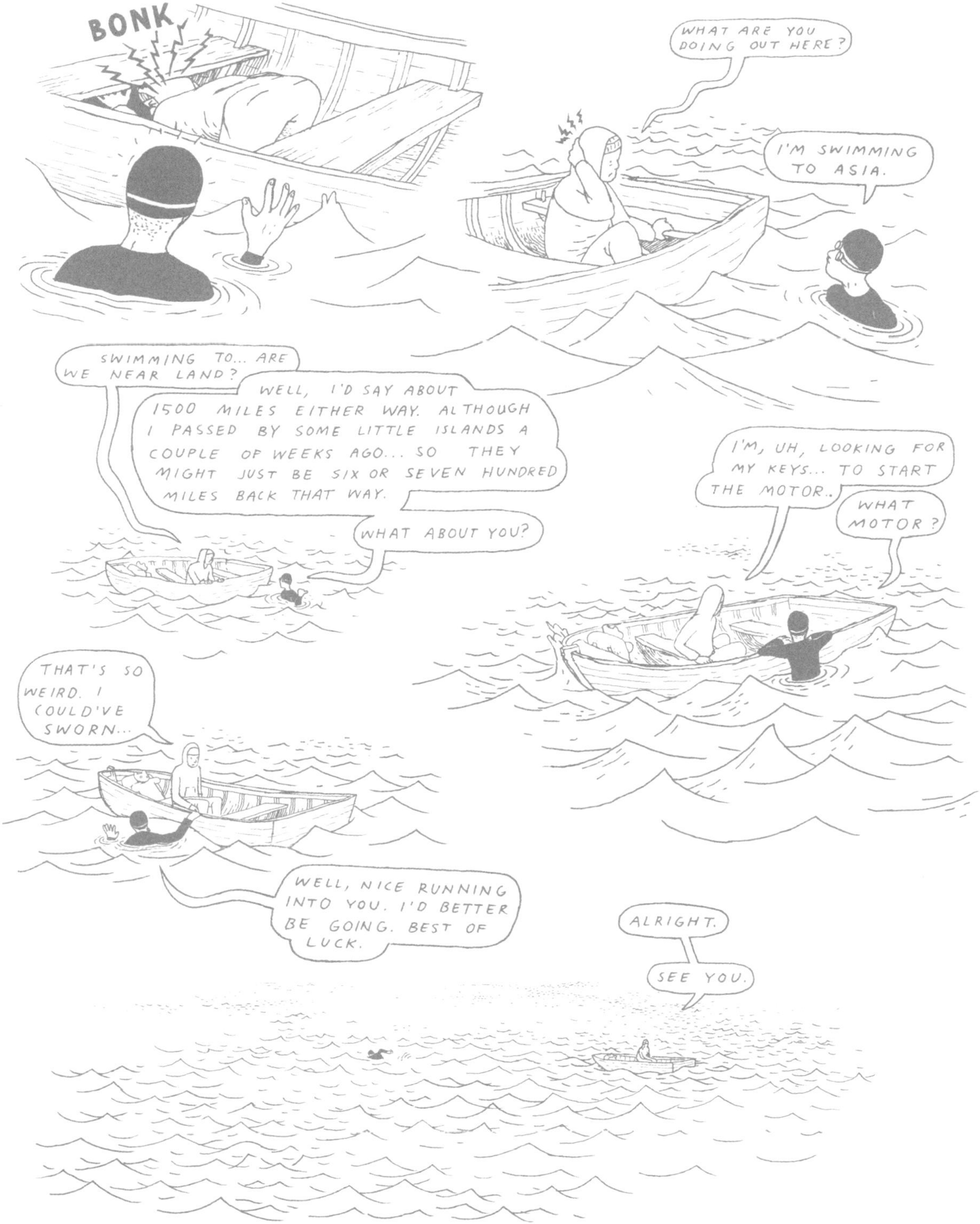
BONK
WHAT ARE YOU DOING OUT HERE?
I'M SWIMMING TO ASIA.
SWIMMING TO... ARE WE NEAR LAND?
WELL, I'D SAY ABOUT 1500 MILES EITHER WAY. ALTHOUGH I PASSED BY SOME LITTLE ISLANDS A COUPLE OF WEEKS AGO... SO THEY MIGHT JUST BE SIX OR SEVEN HUNDRED MILES BACK THAT WAY.
WHAT ABOUT YOU?
I'M, UH, LOOKING FOR MY KEYS... TO START THE MOTOR..
WHAT MOTOR?
THAT'S SO WEIRD. I COULD'VE SWORN...
WELL, NICE RUNNING INTO YOU. I'D BETTER BE GOING. BEST OF LUCK.
ALRIGHT.
SEE YOU.

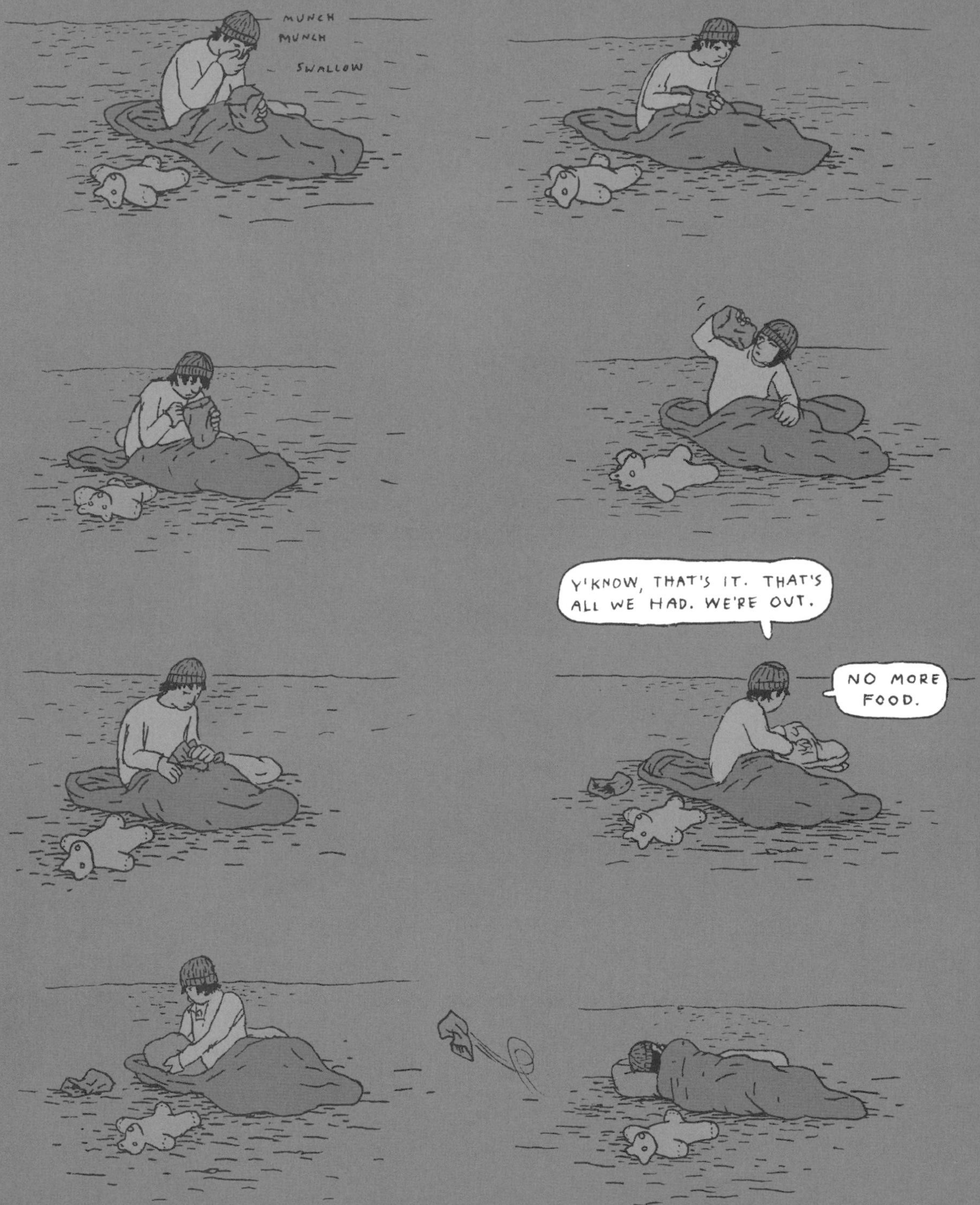
MUNCH
MUNCH
SWALLOW
Y'KNOW, THAT'S IT. THAT'S ALL WE HAD. WE'RE OUT.
NO MORE FOOD.

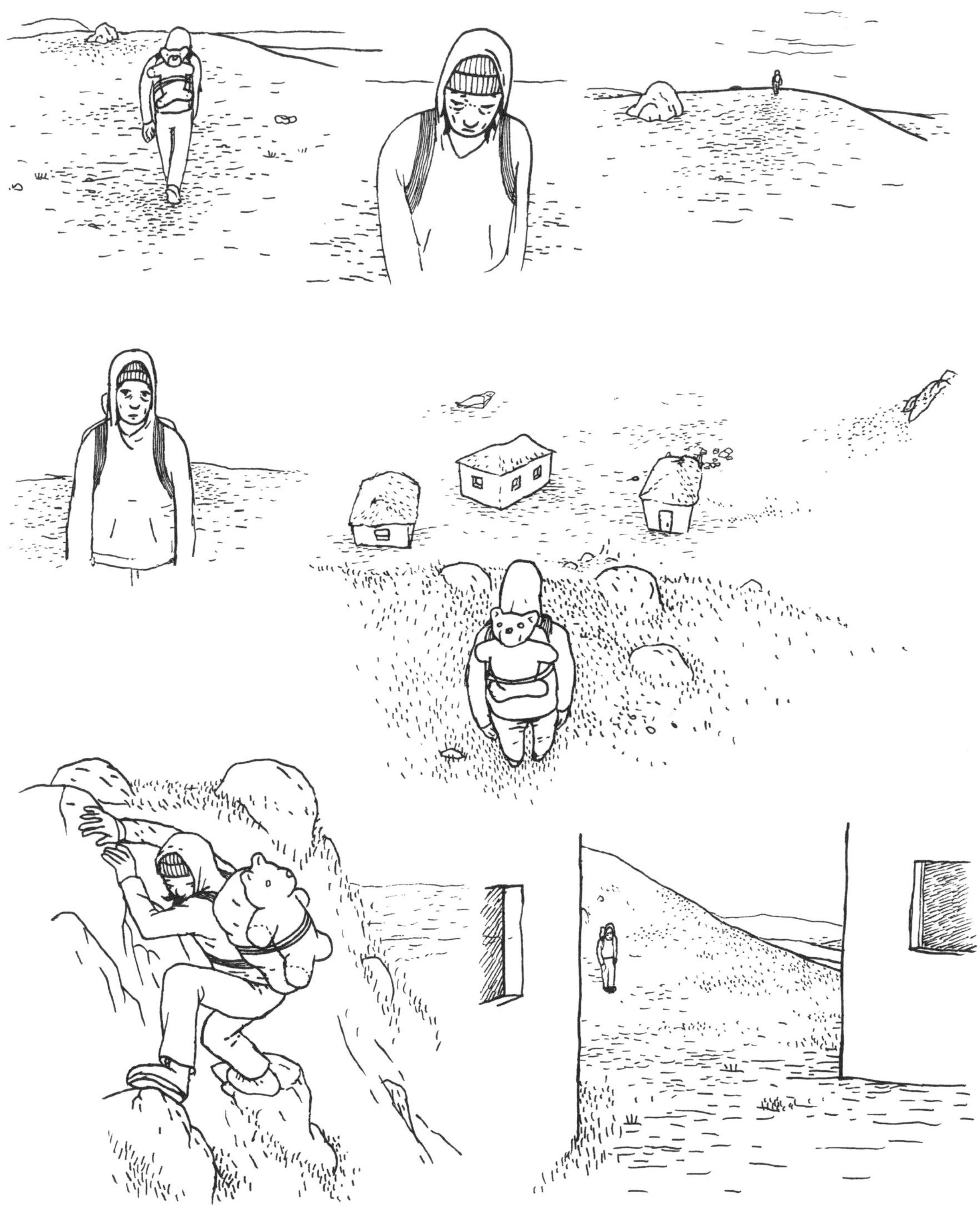

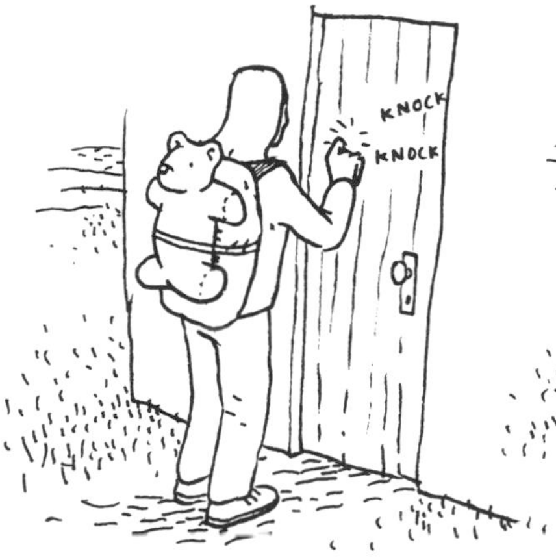
KNOCK
KNOCK

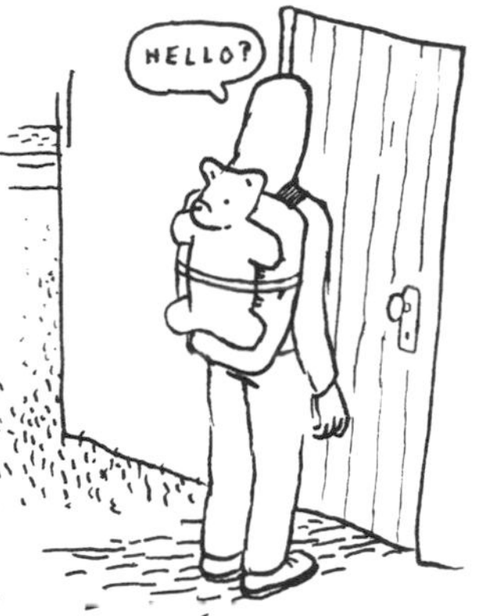
HELLO?

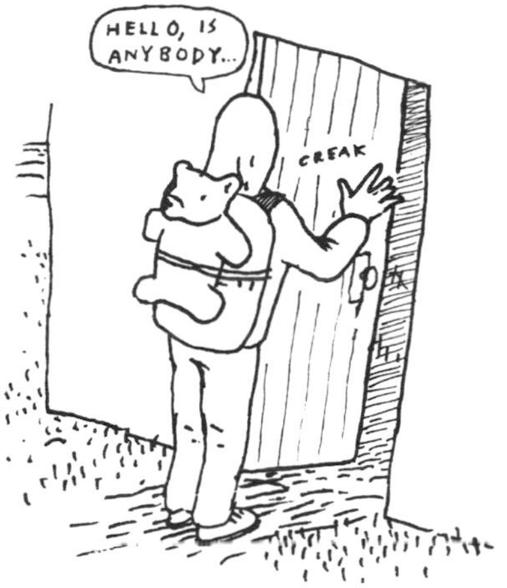
HELLO, IS ANYBODY...
CREAK

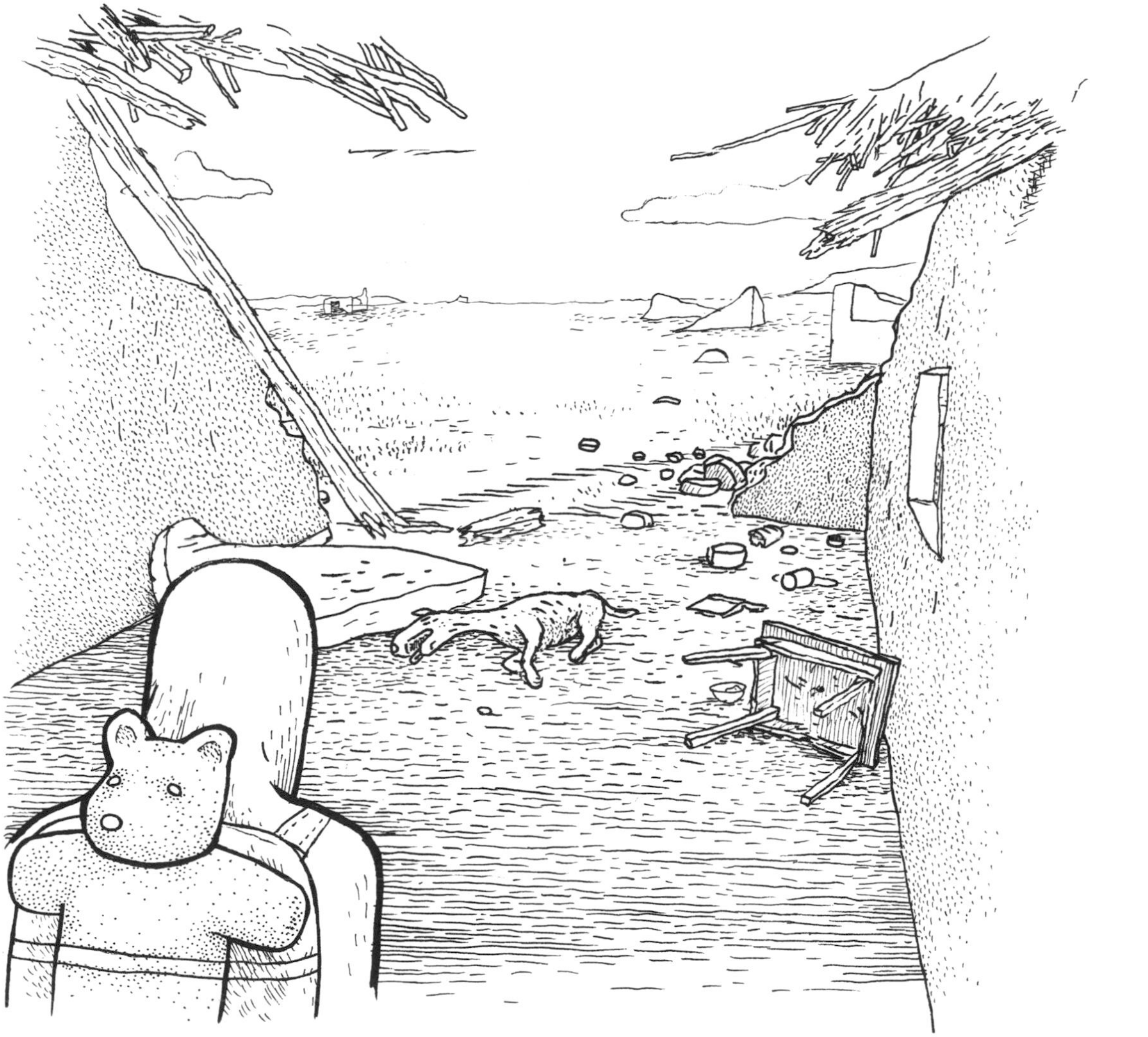

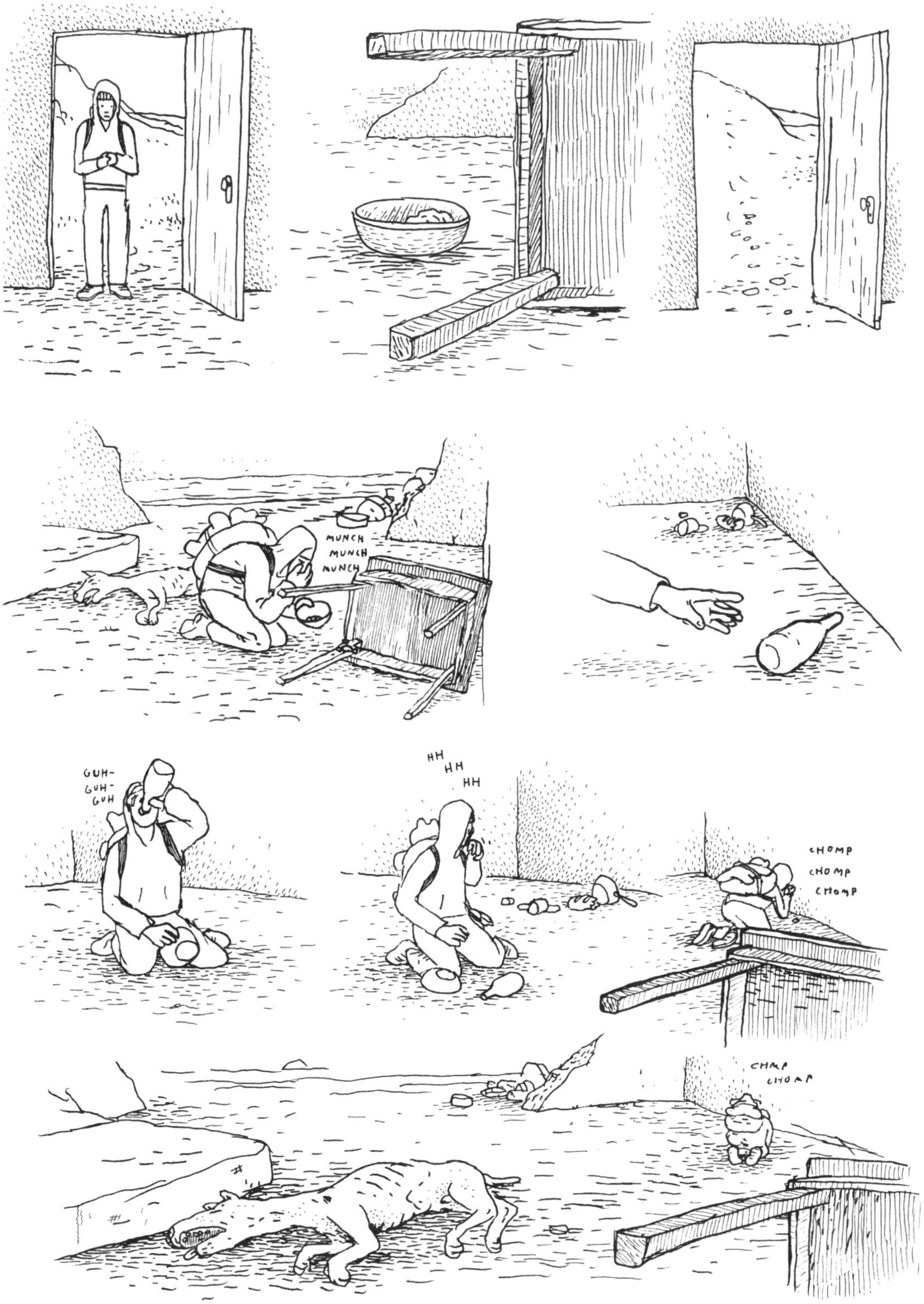
MUNCH
MUNCH
MUNCH
GUH-
GUH-
GUH
HH
HH
HH
CHOMP
CHOMP
CHOMP
CHMP
CHOMP

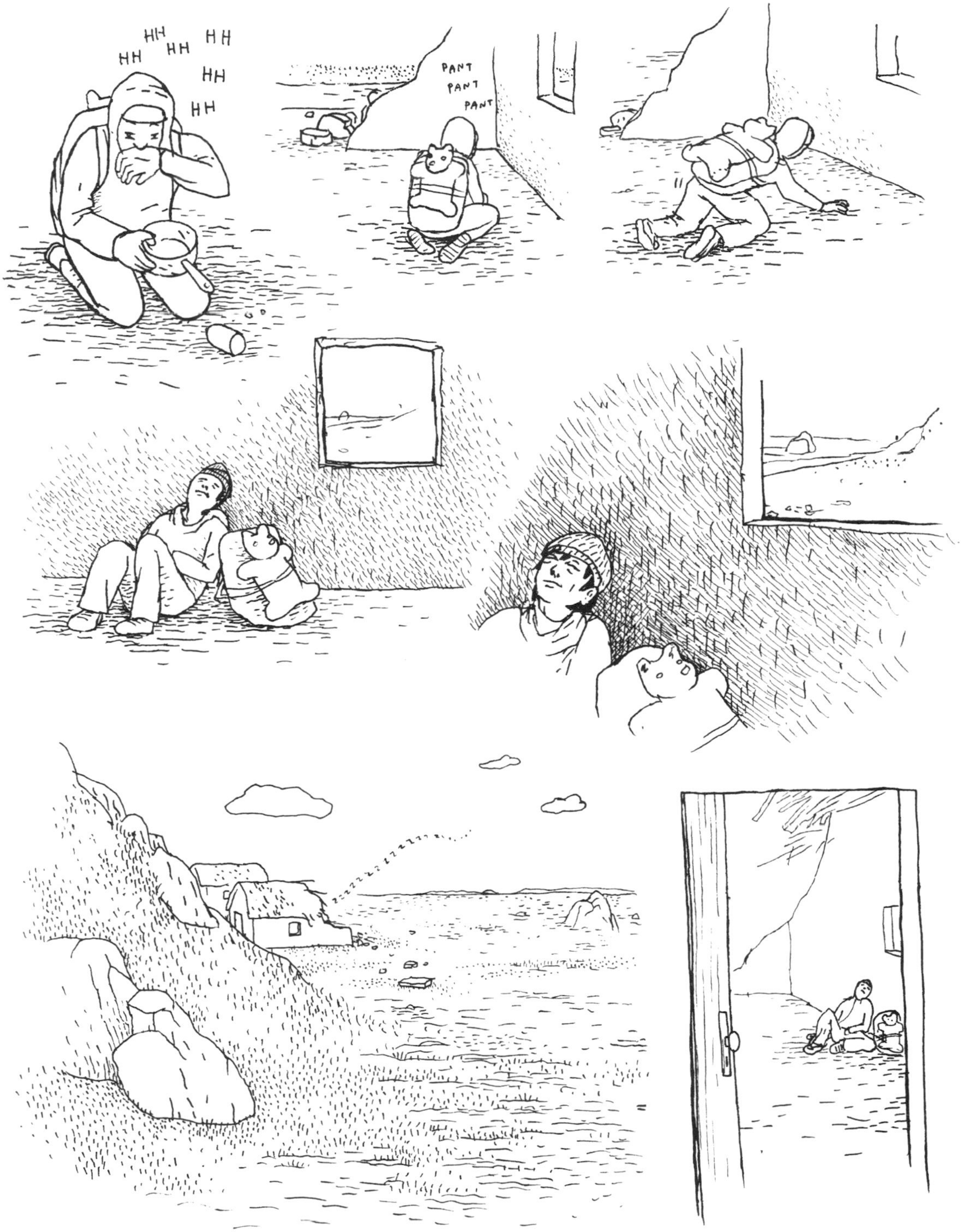
HH HH HH HH
HH
HH
PANT
PANT
PANT

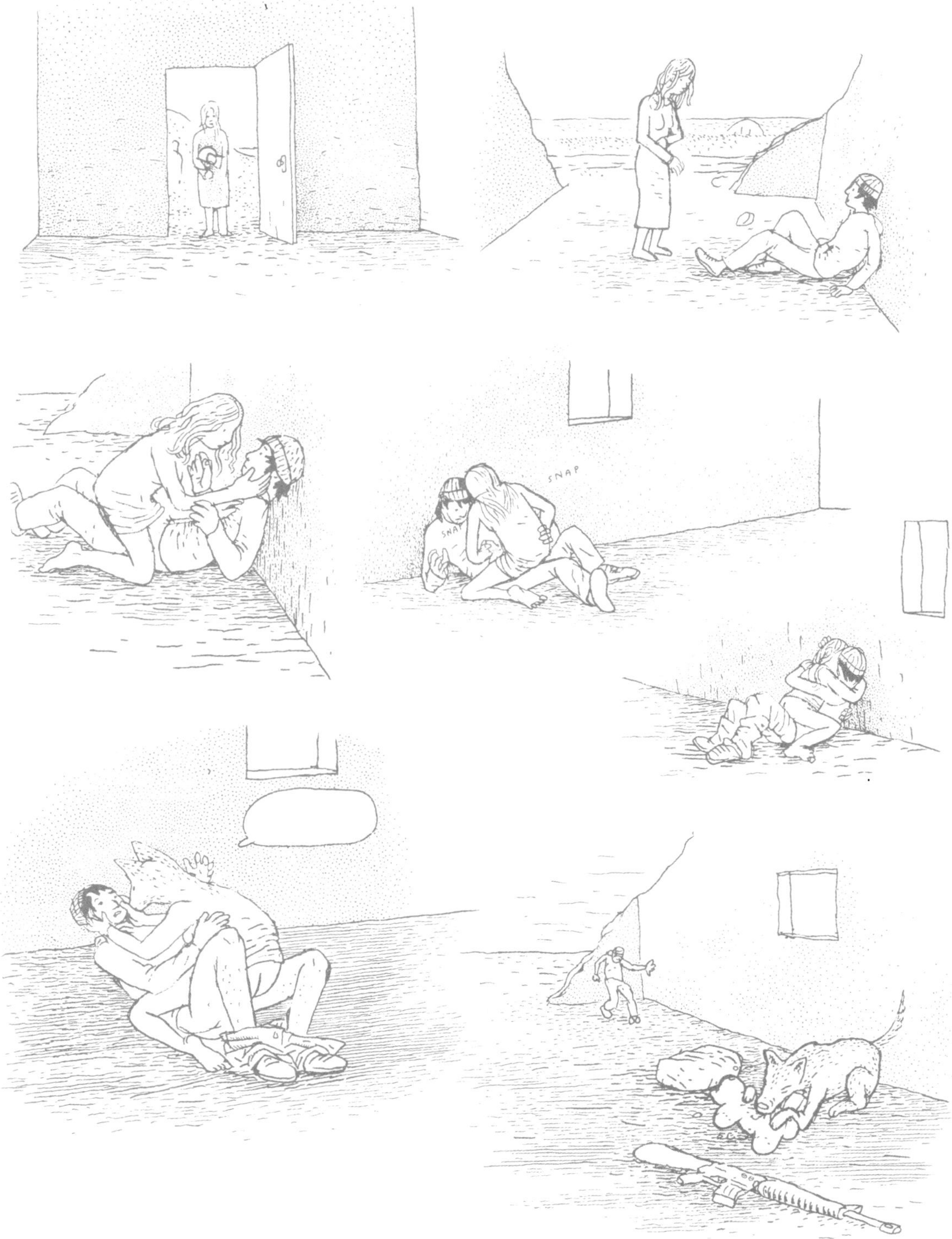
SNAP
SNAP

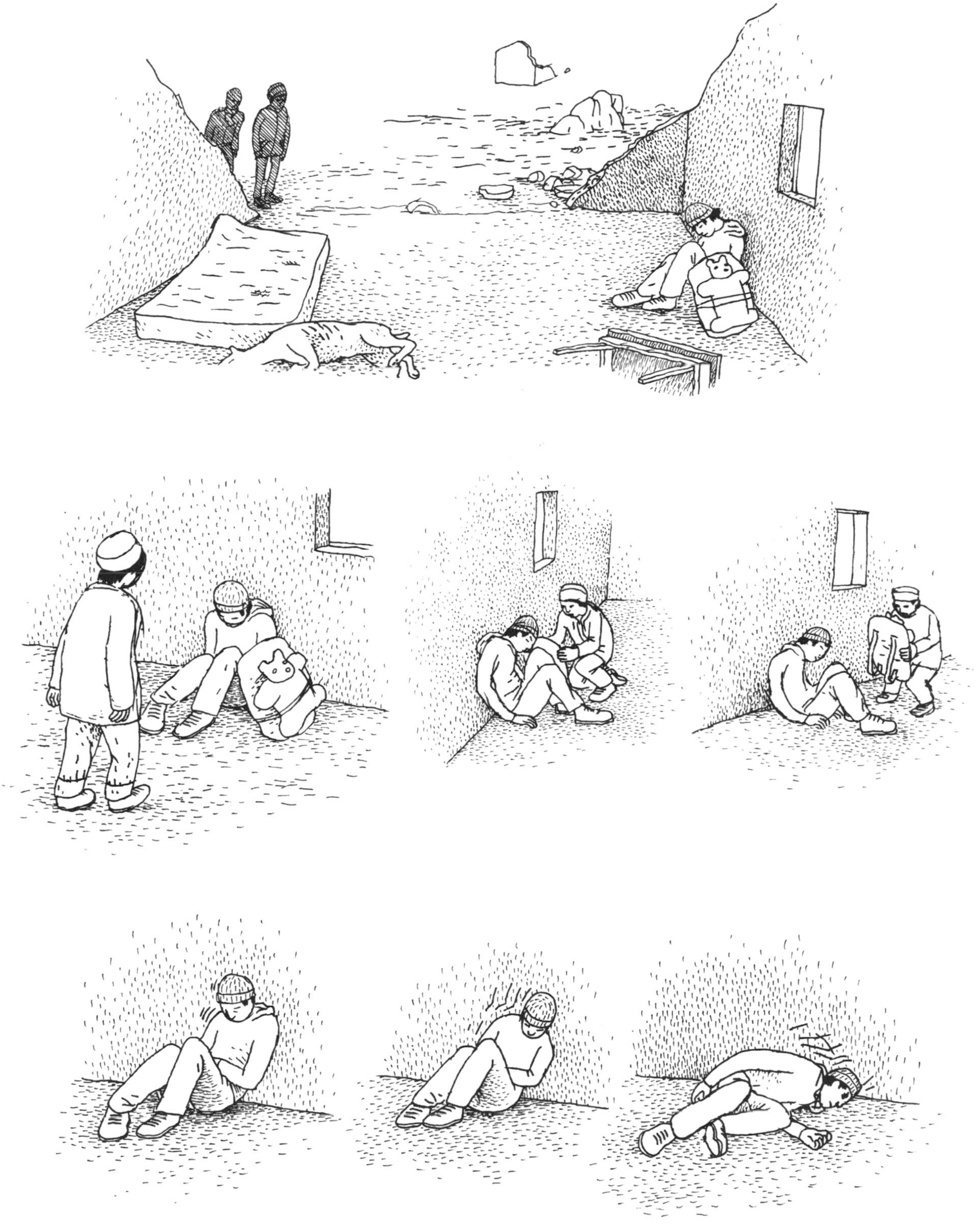

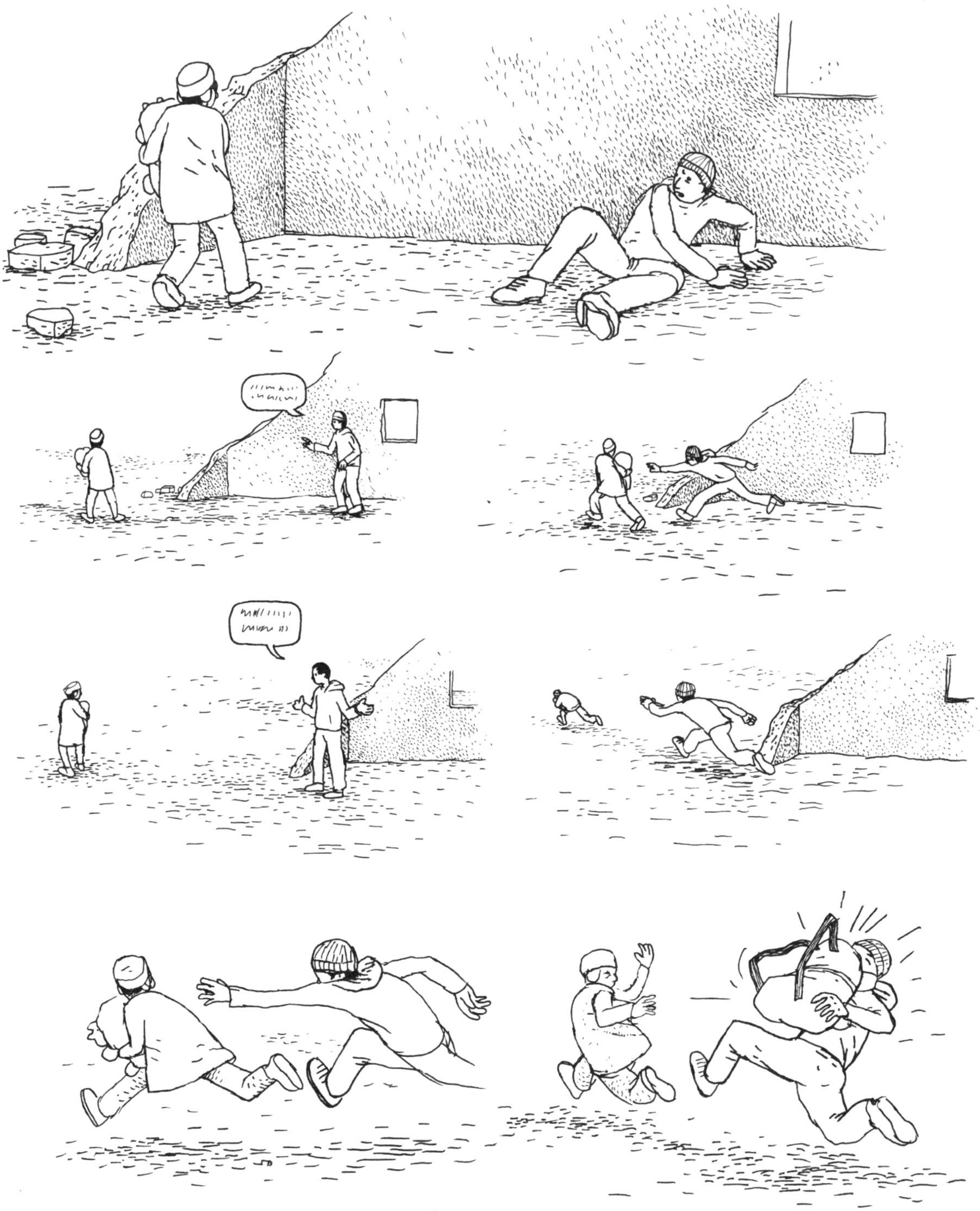

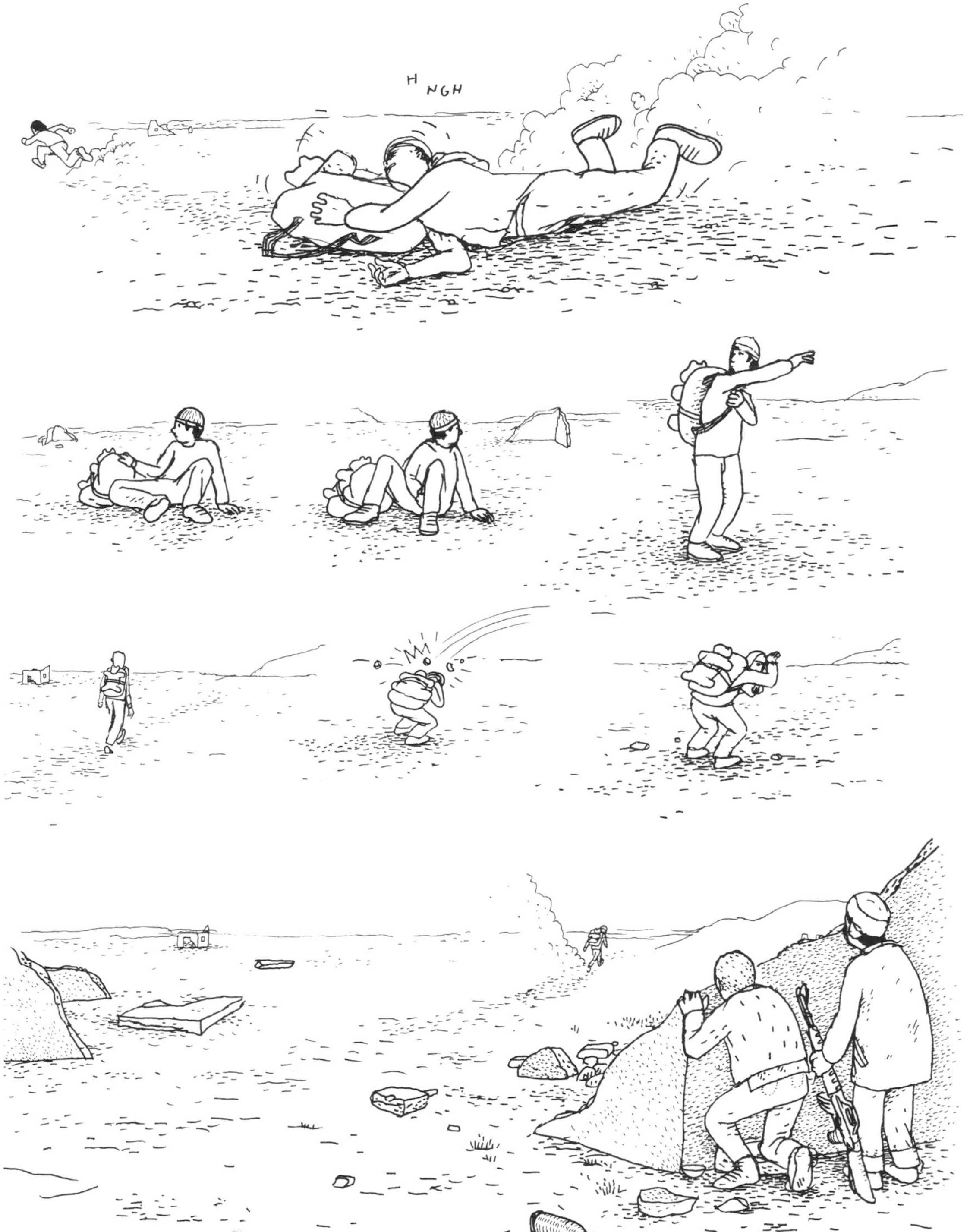
H NGH

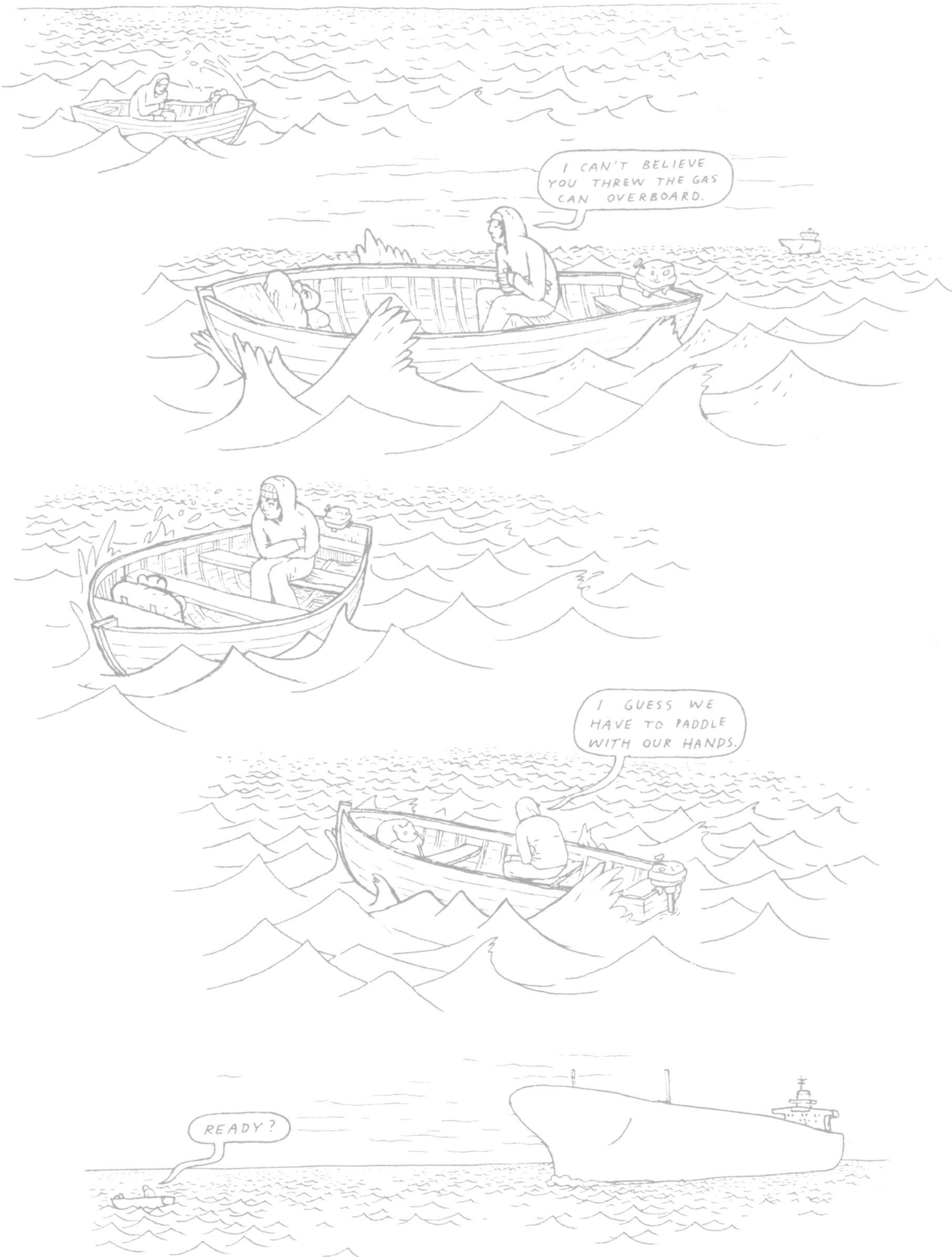
I CAN'T BELIEVE YOU THREW THE GAS CAN OVERBOARD.
I GUESS WE HAVE TO PADDLE WITH OUR HANDS.
READY?

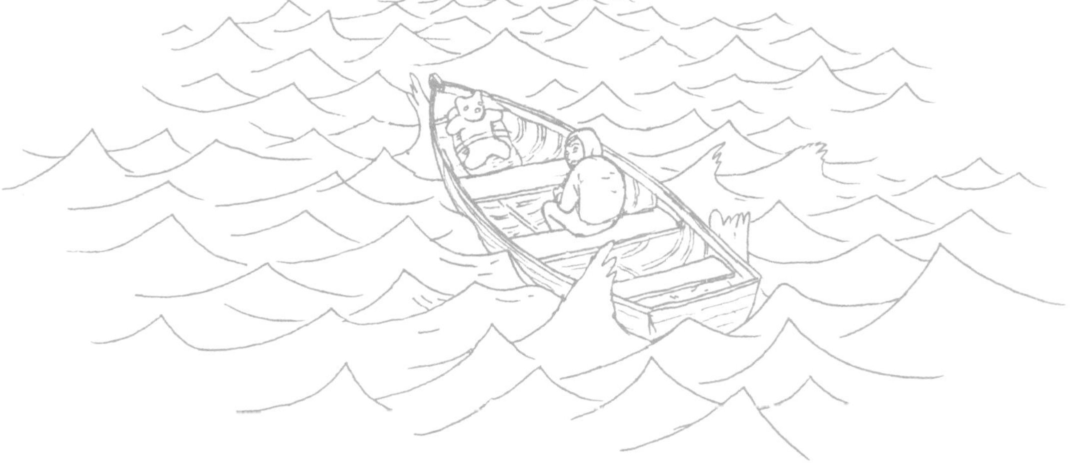

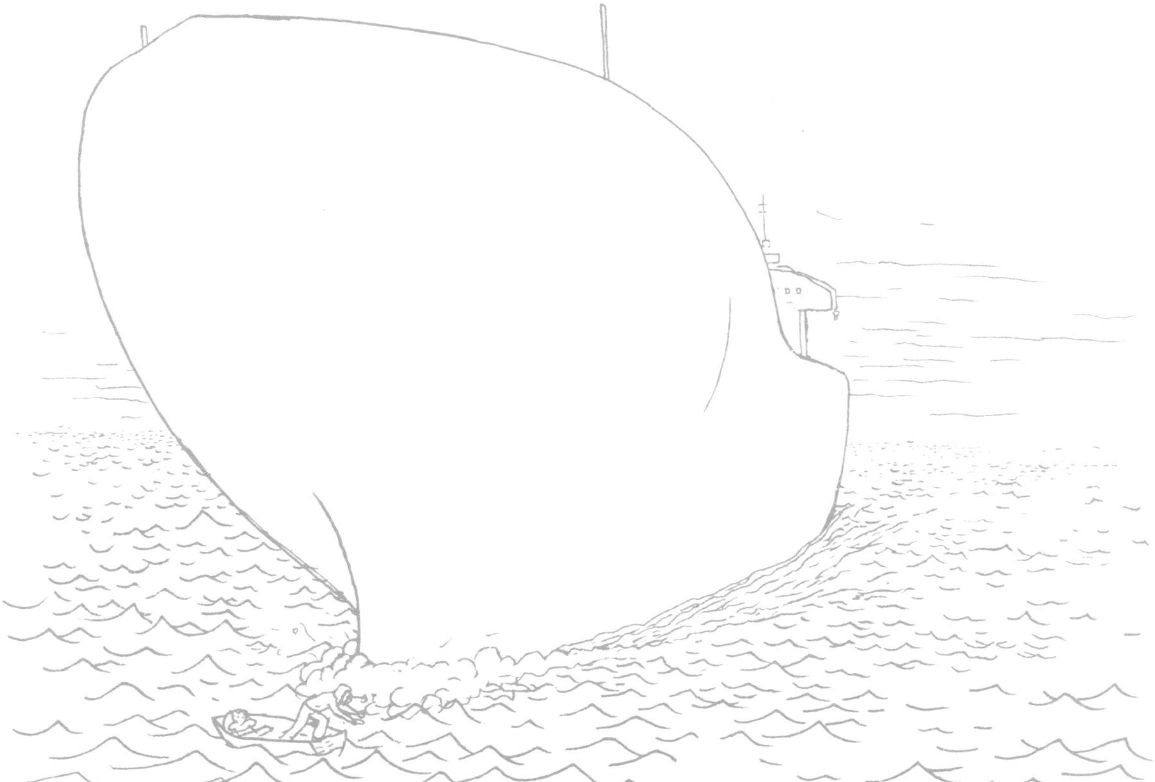

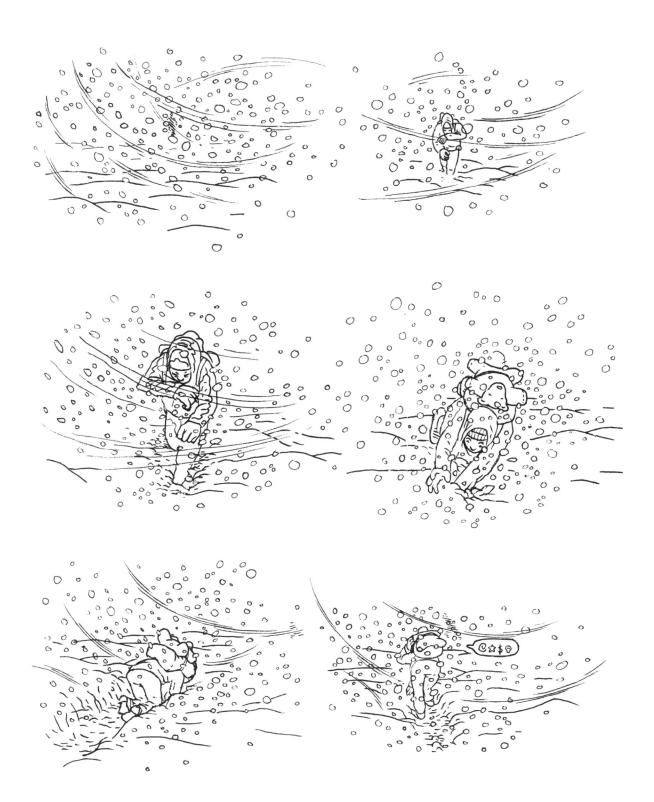

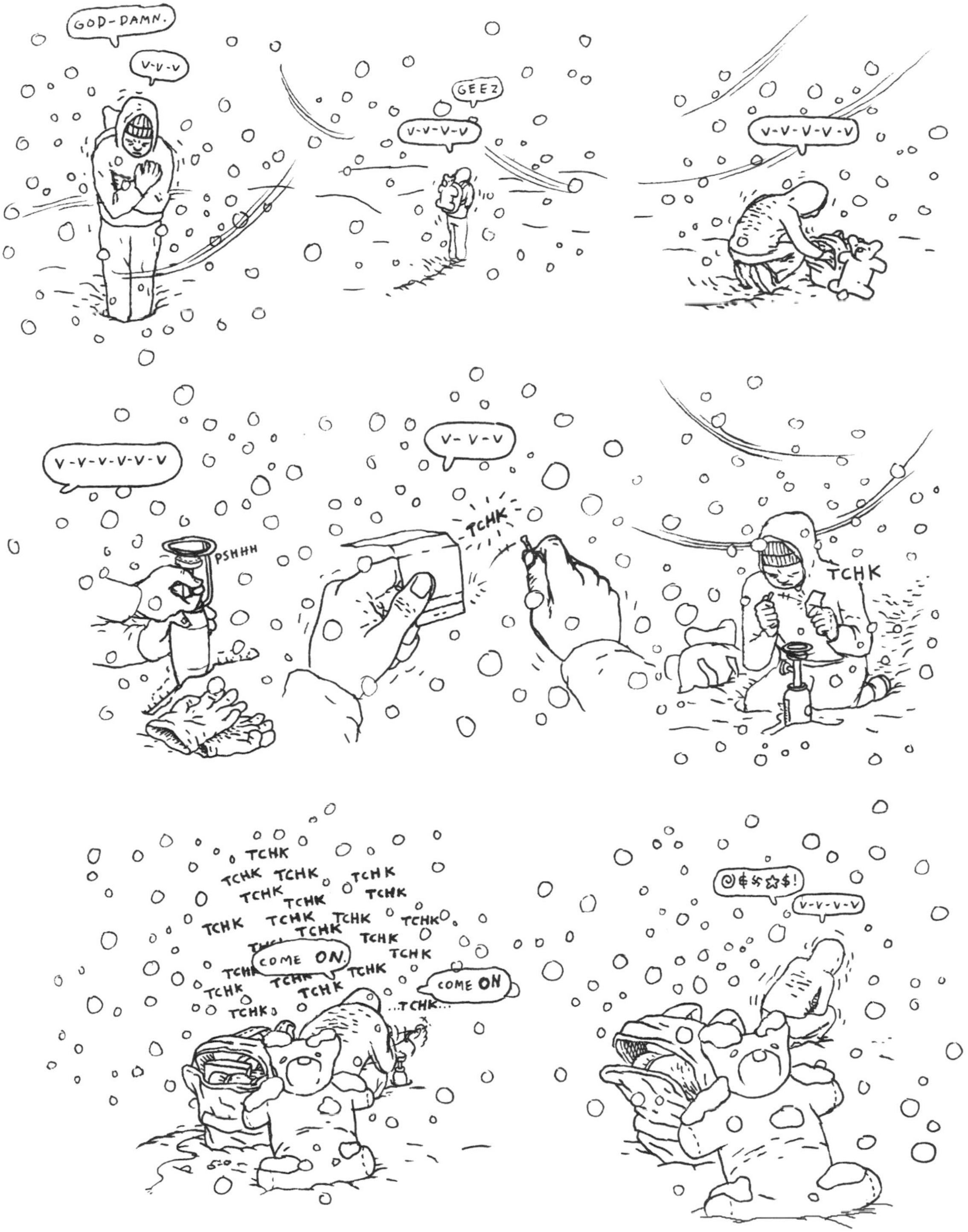
GOD-DAMN.
V-V-V
GEEZ
V-V-V-V-V
V-V-V-V-V-V
V-V-V-V-V-V-V
PSHHH
V-V-V
TCHK
TCHK
TCHK TCHK TCHK TCHK TCHK TCHK TCHK TCHK TCHK TCHK TCHK TCHK TCHK TCHK TCHK TCHK TCHK
COME ON.
COME ON
...TCHK...
@$%☆$!
V-V-V-V

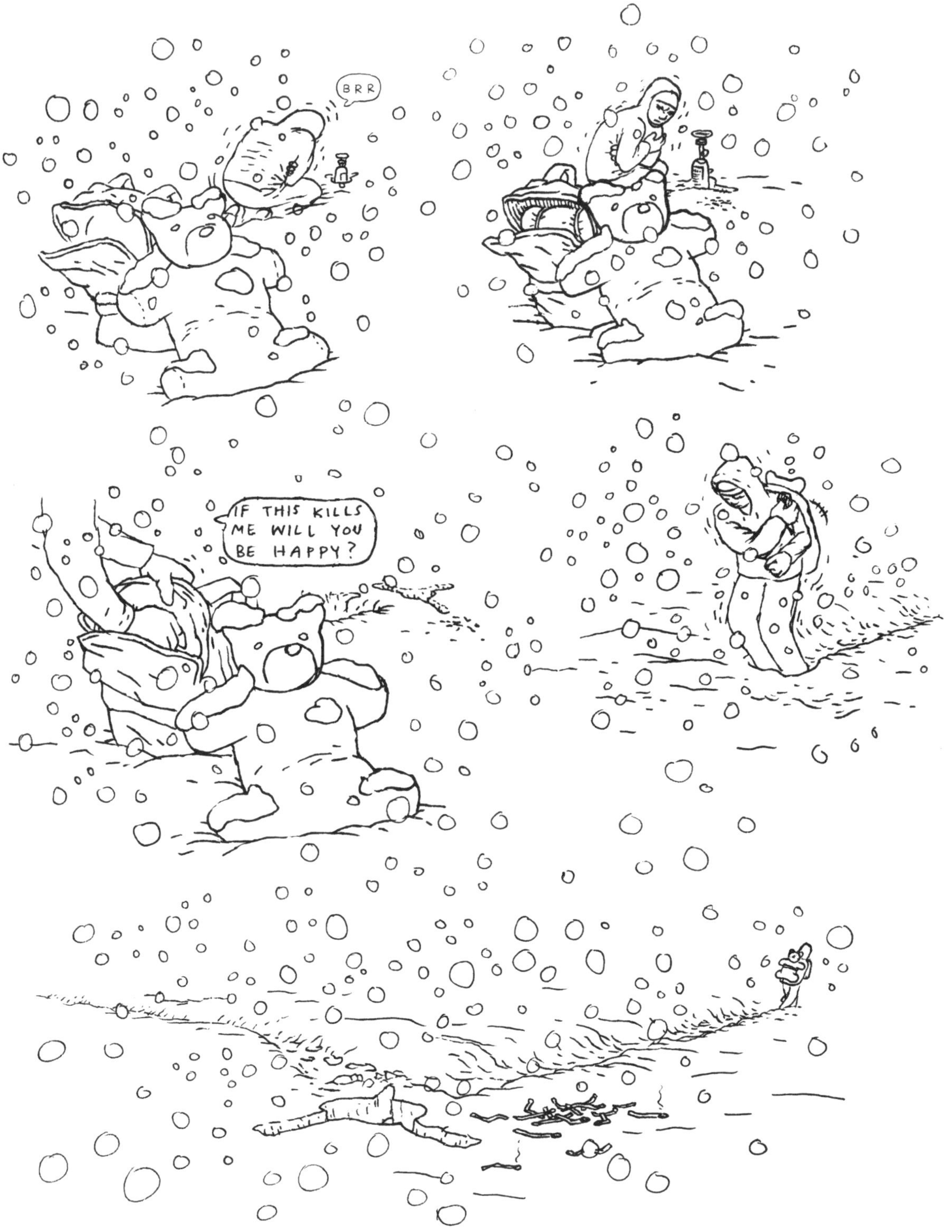
BRR
IF THIS KILLS ME WILL YOU BE HAPPY?

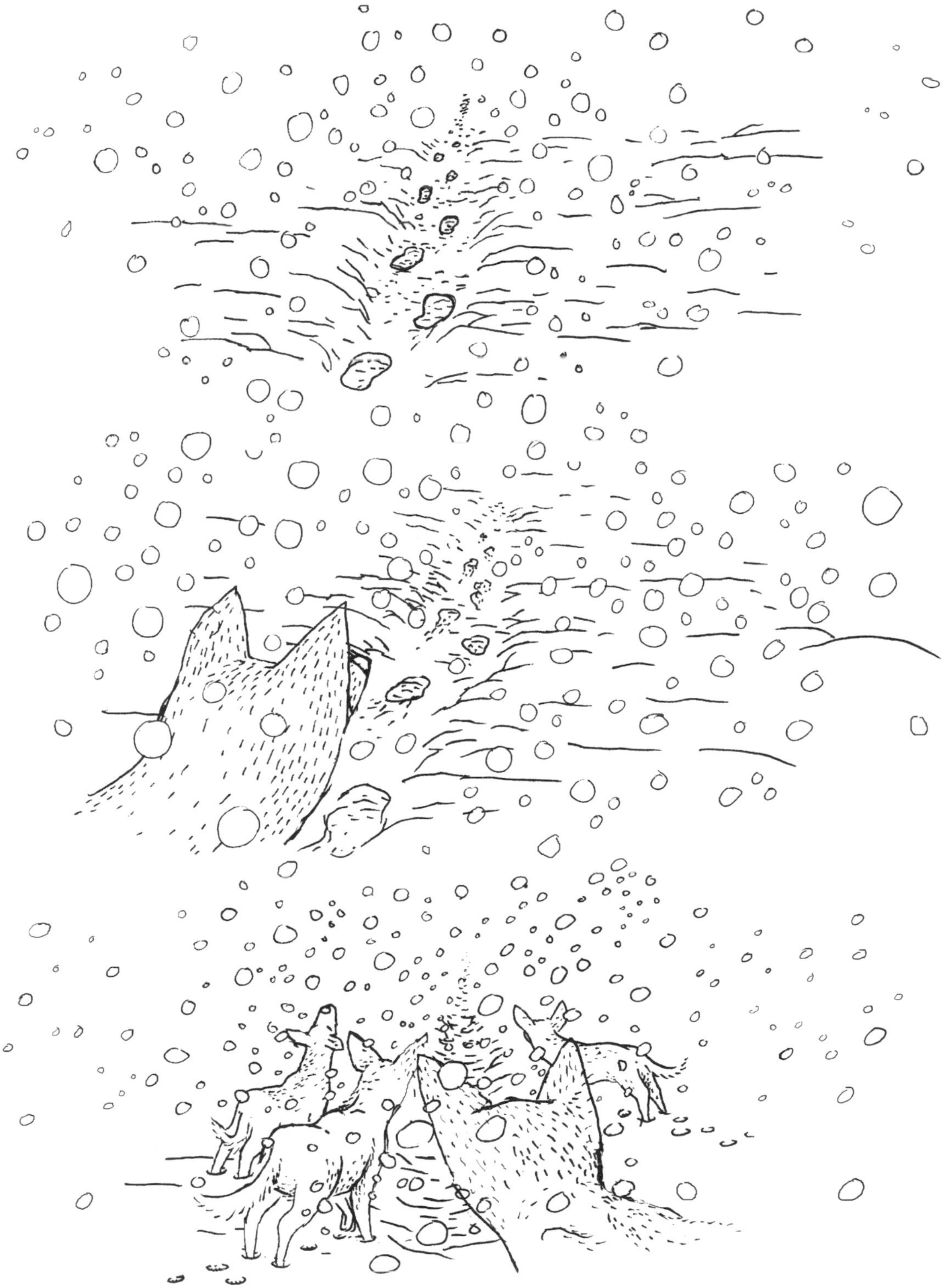

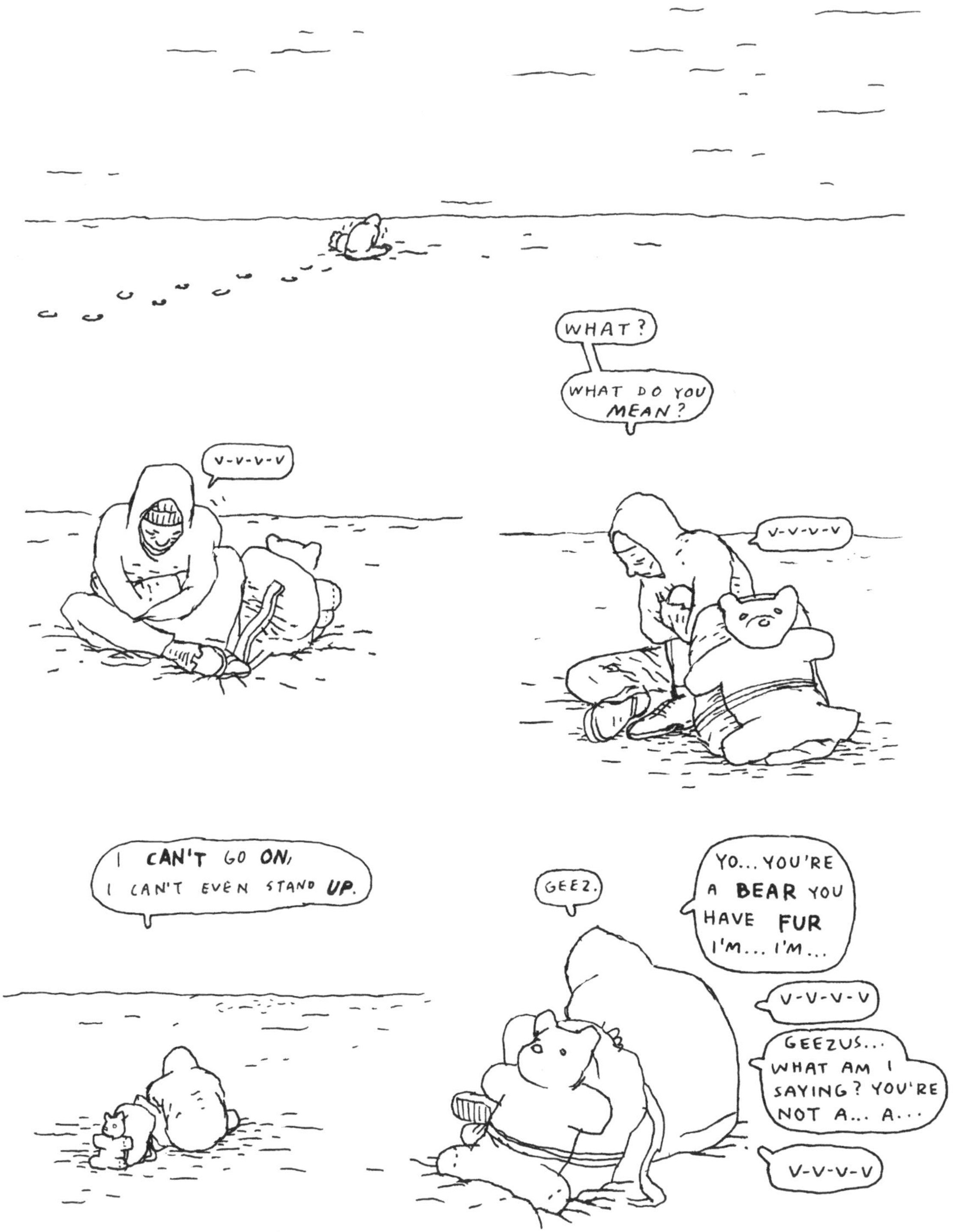
V-V-V-V
WHAT?
WHAT DO YOU MEAN?
V-V-V-V
I CAN'T GO ON, I CAN'T EVEN STAND UP.
GEEZ.
YO... YOU'RE A BEAR YOU HAVE FUR I'M... I'M...
V-V-V-V
GEEZUS... WHAT AM I SAYING? YOU'RE NOT A... A...
V-V-V-V

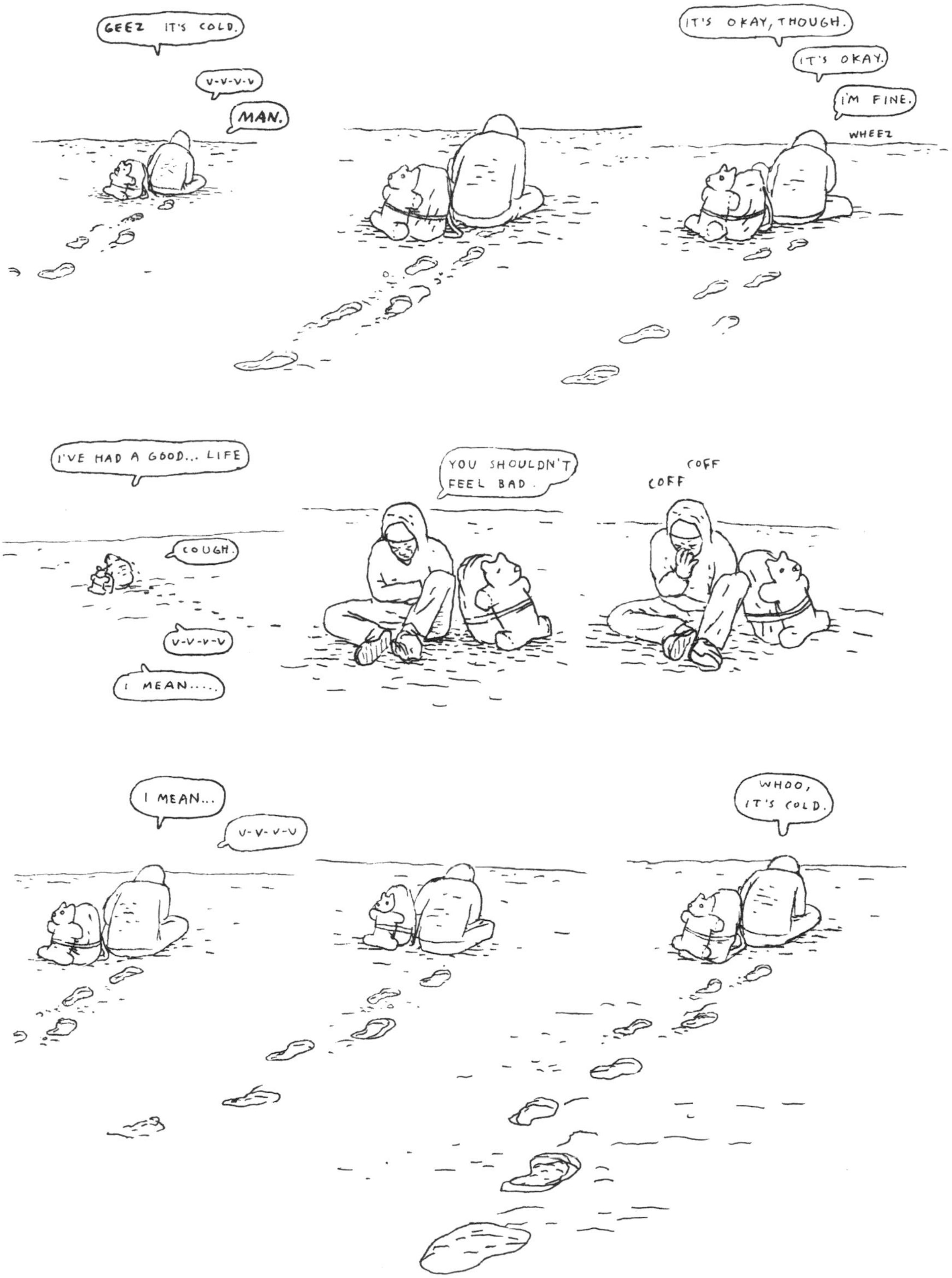
GEEZ IT'S COLD.
V-V-V-V
MAN.
IT'S OKAY, THOUGH.
IT'S OKAY.
I'M FINE.
WHEEZ
I'VE HAD A GOOD... LIFE
COUGH.
V-V-V-V
I MEAN.....
YOU SHOULDN'T FEEL BAD.
COFF
COFF
I MEAN...
V-V-V-V
WHOO, IT'S COLD.

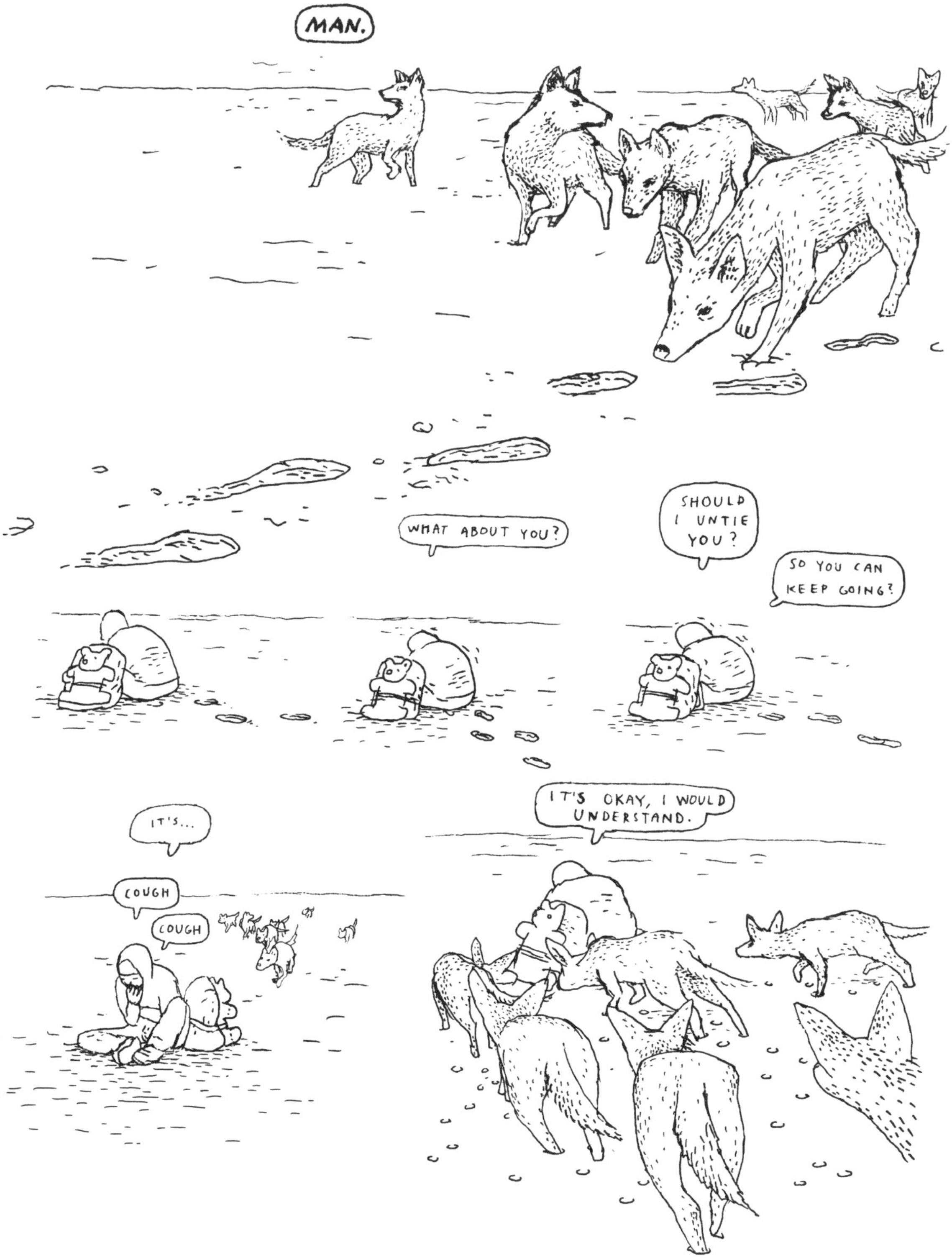
MAN.
WHAT ABOUT YOU?
SHOULD I UNTIE YOU?
SO YOU CAN KEEP GOING?
IT'S...
COUGH
COUGH
IT'S OKAY, I WOULD UNDERSTAND.

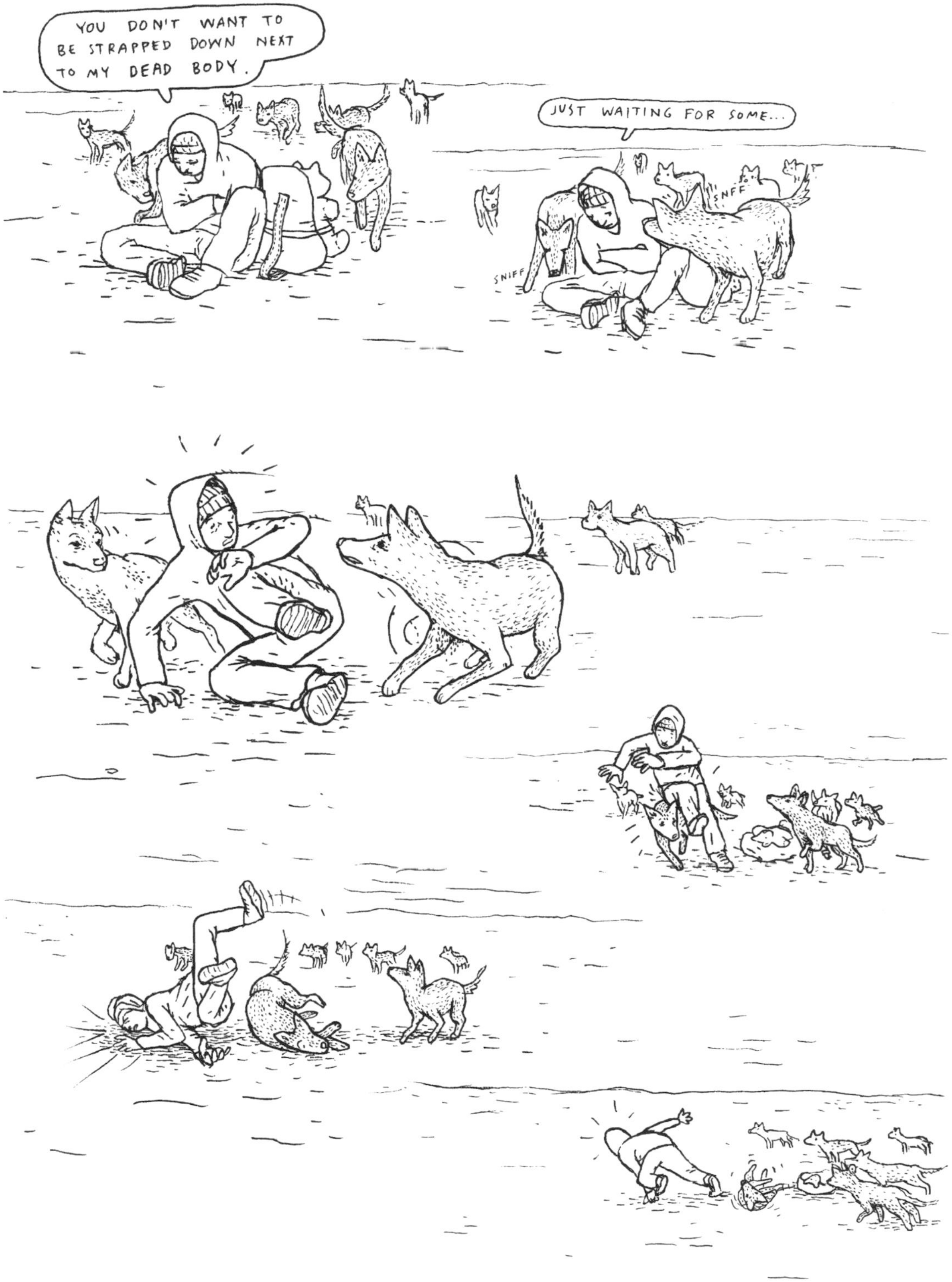
YOU DON'T WANT TO BE STRAPPED DOWN NEXT TO MY DEAD BODY.
JUST WAITING FOR SOME...
SNIFF
SNFF

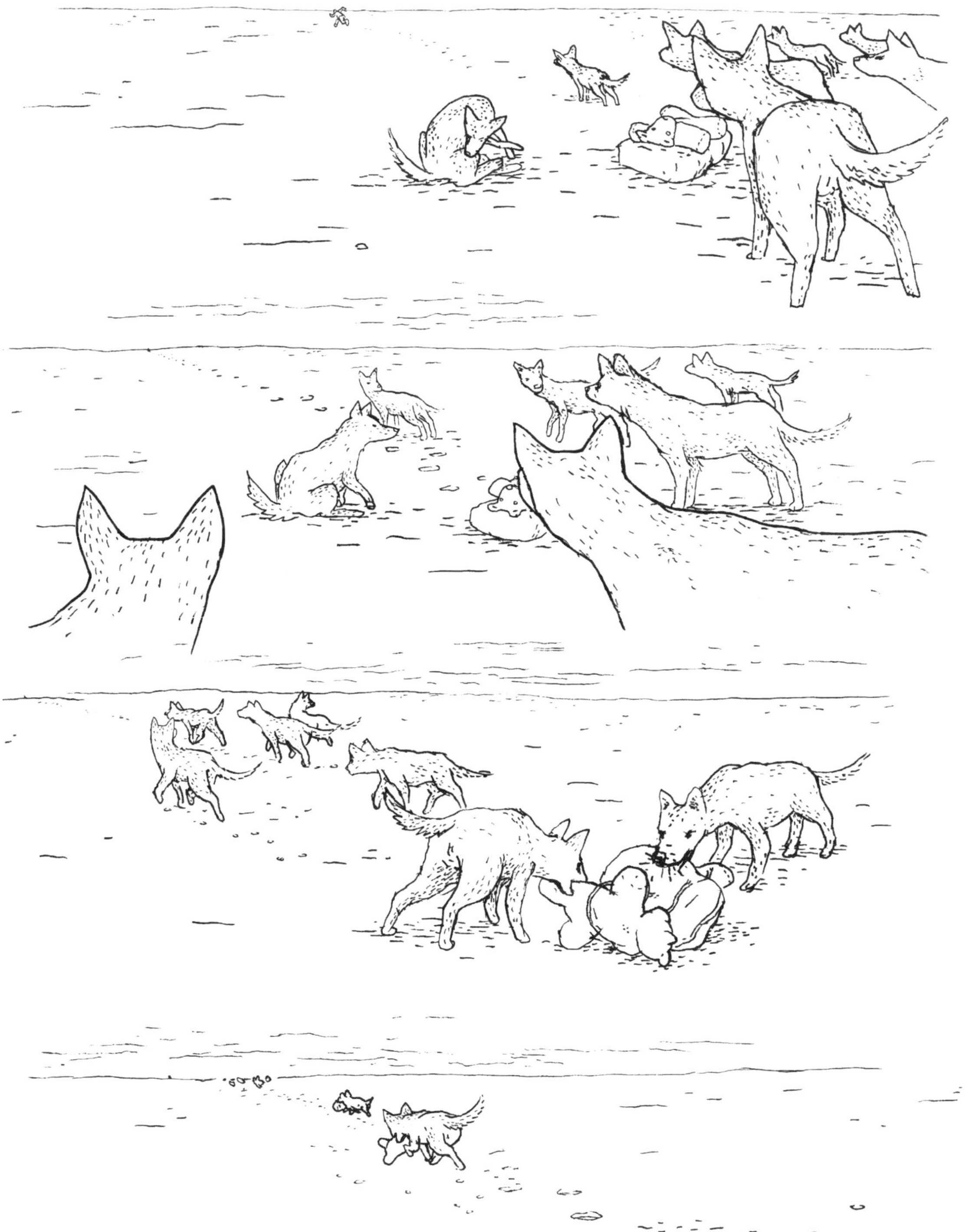

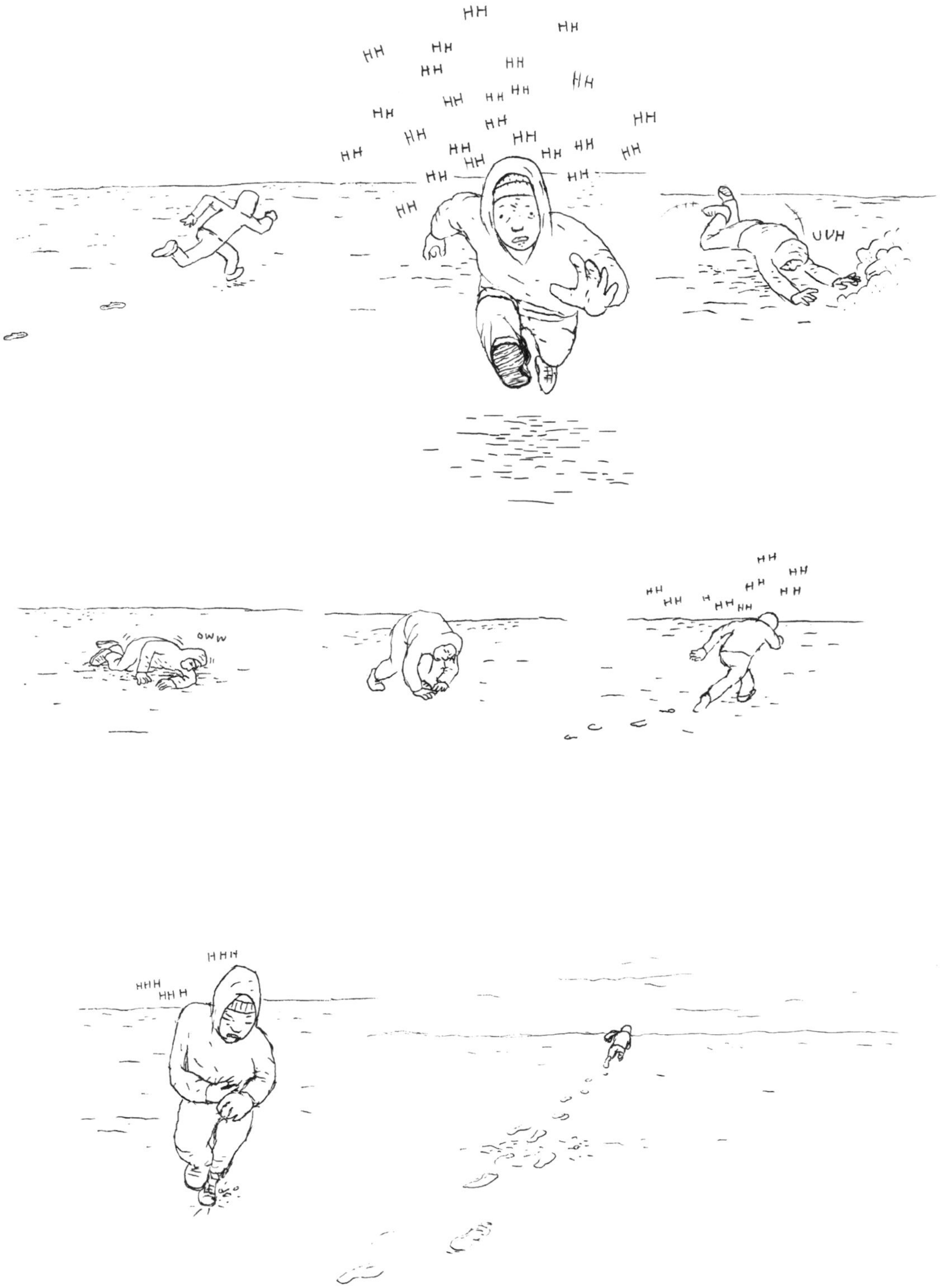
HH HH HH HH HH HH HH HH HH HH HH HH HH HH HH HH HH HH HH HH HH HH HH HH
UUH
OWW
HH HH HH H HH HH HH HH HH HH
HHH HHH HHH

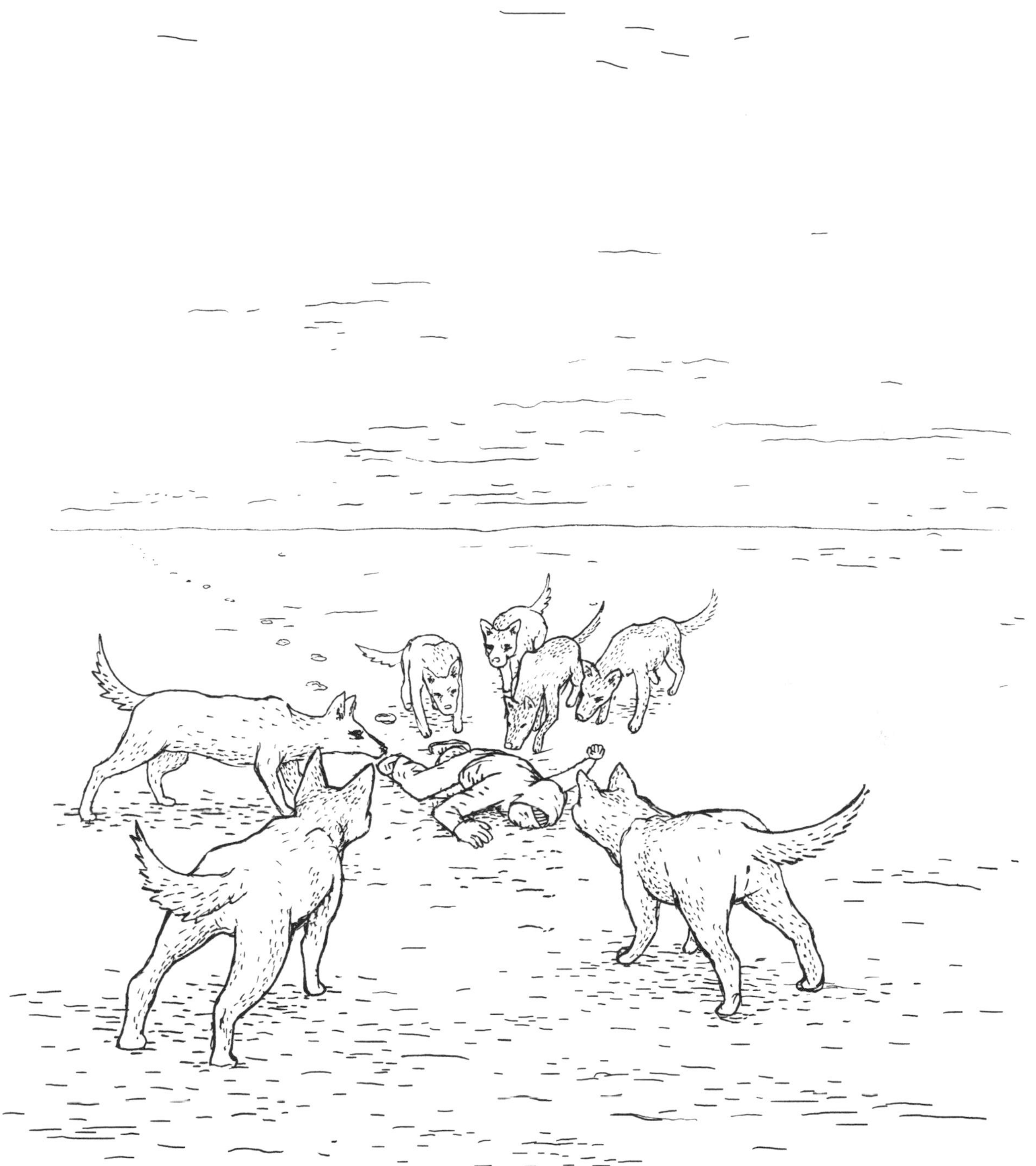

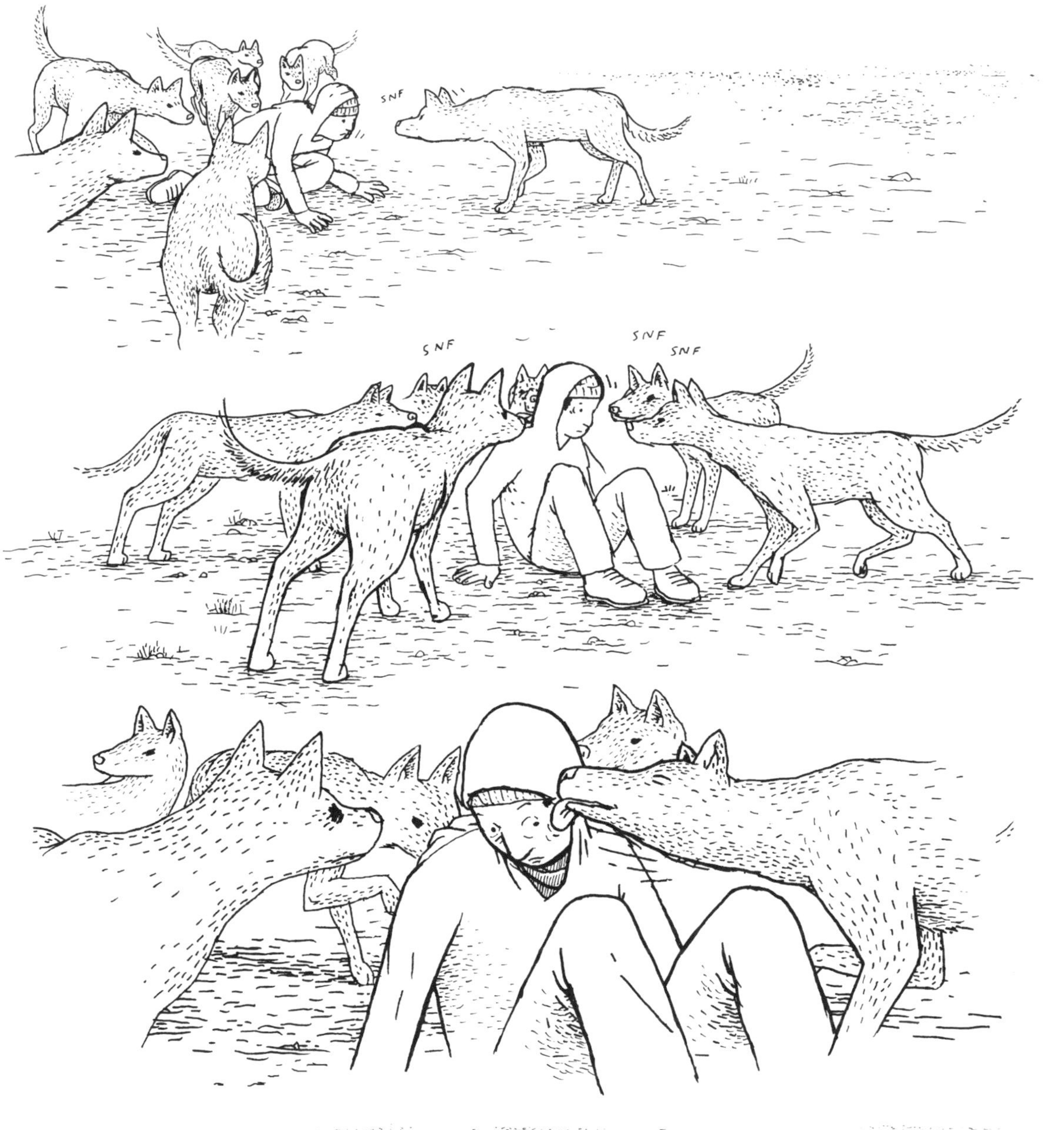
SNF
SNF
SNF
SNF

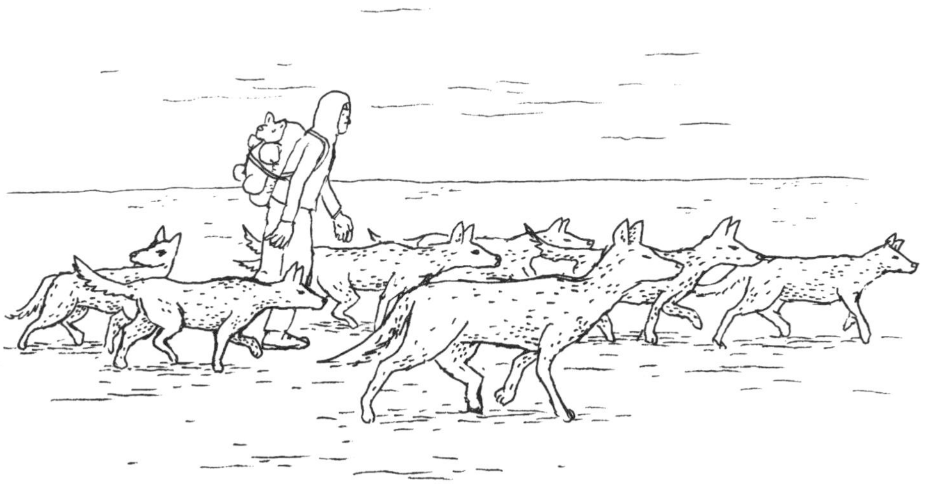

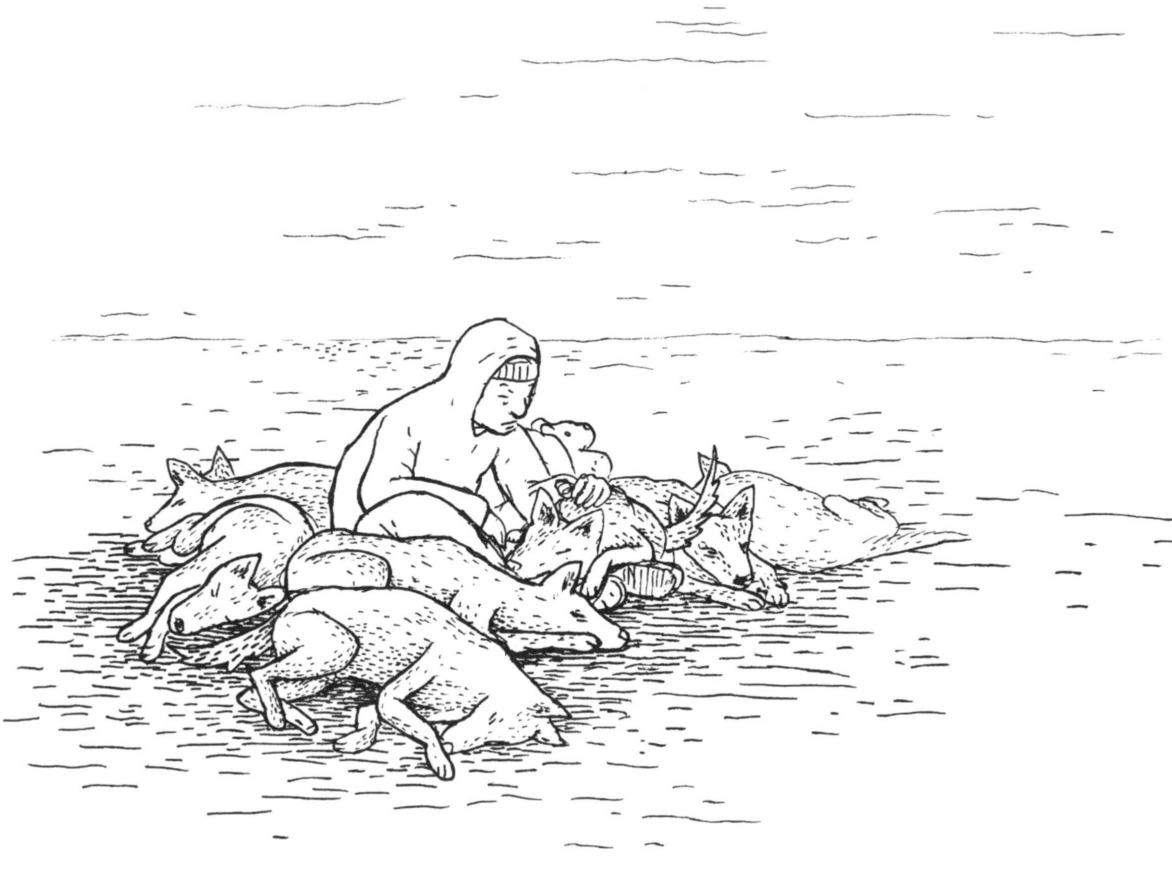

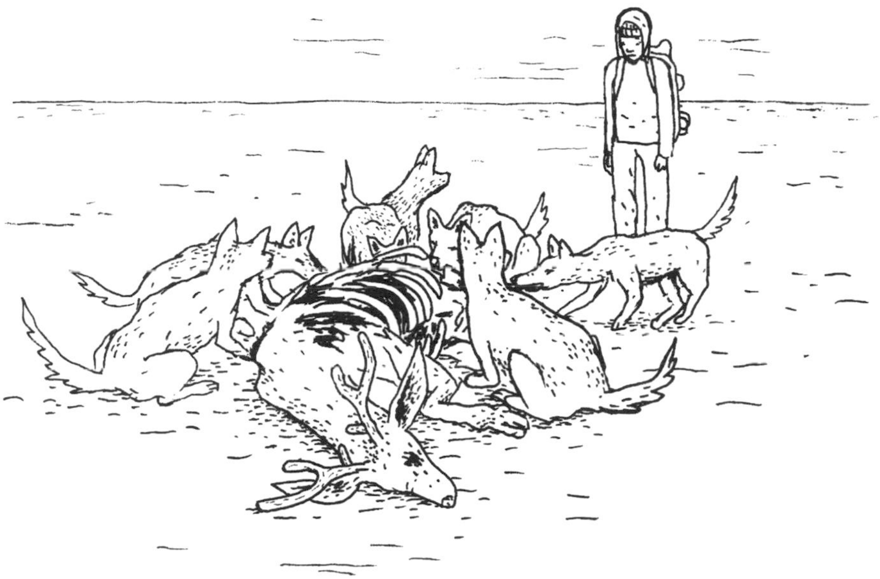

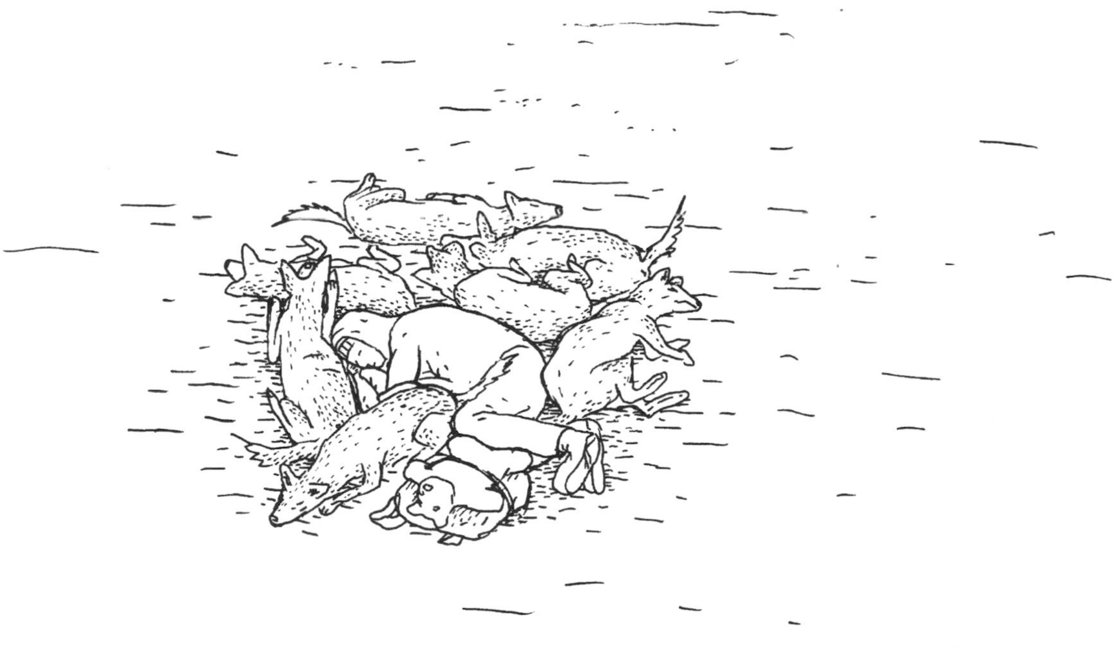

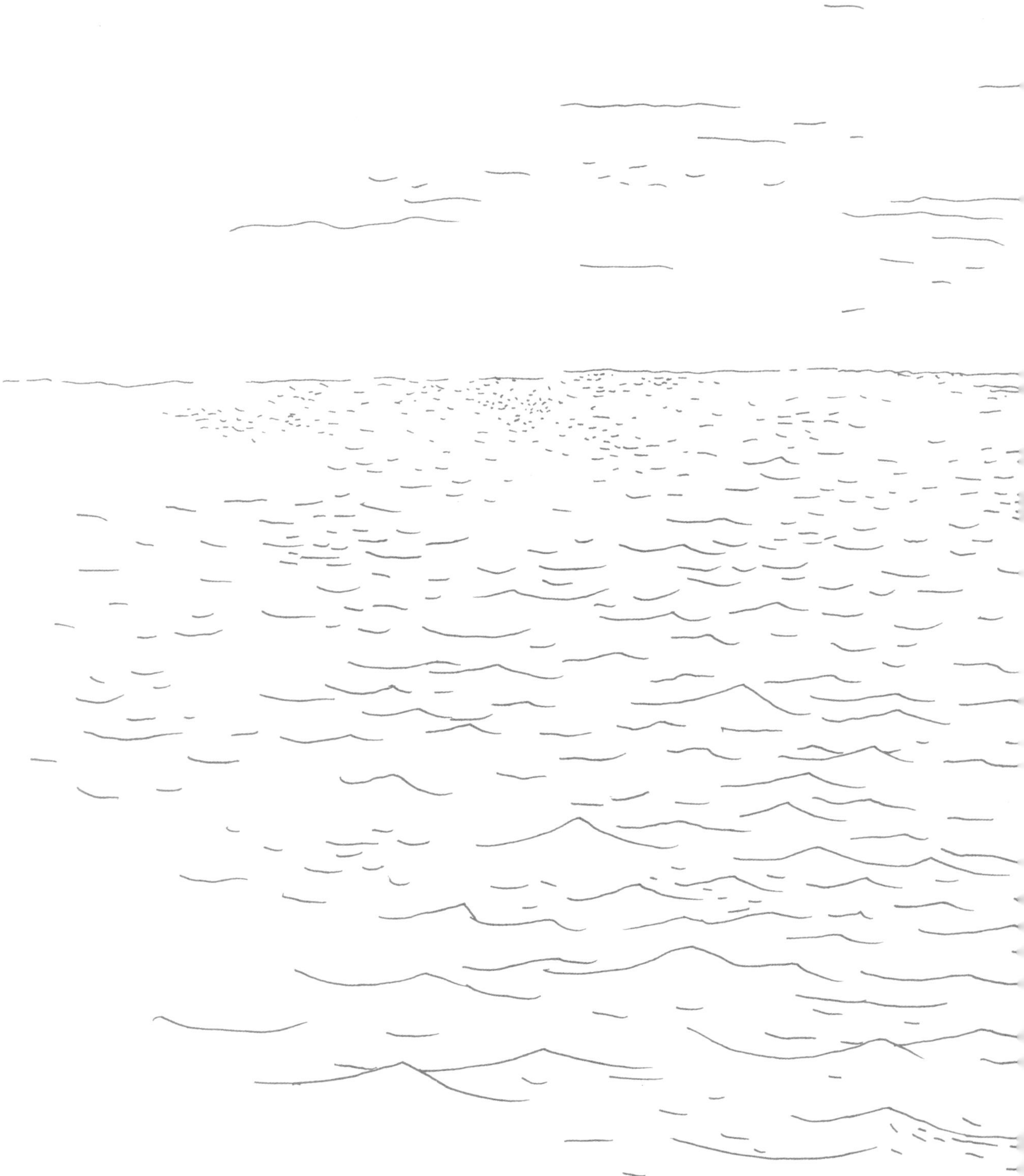

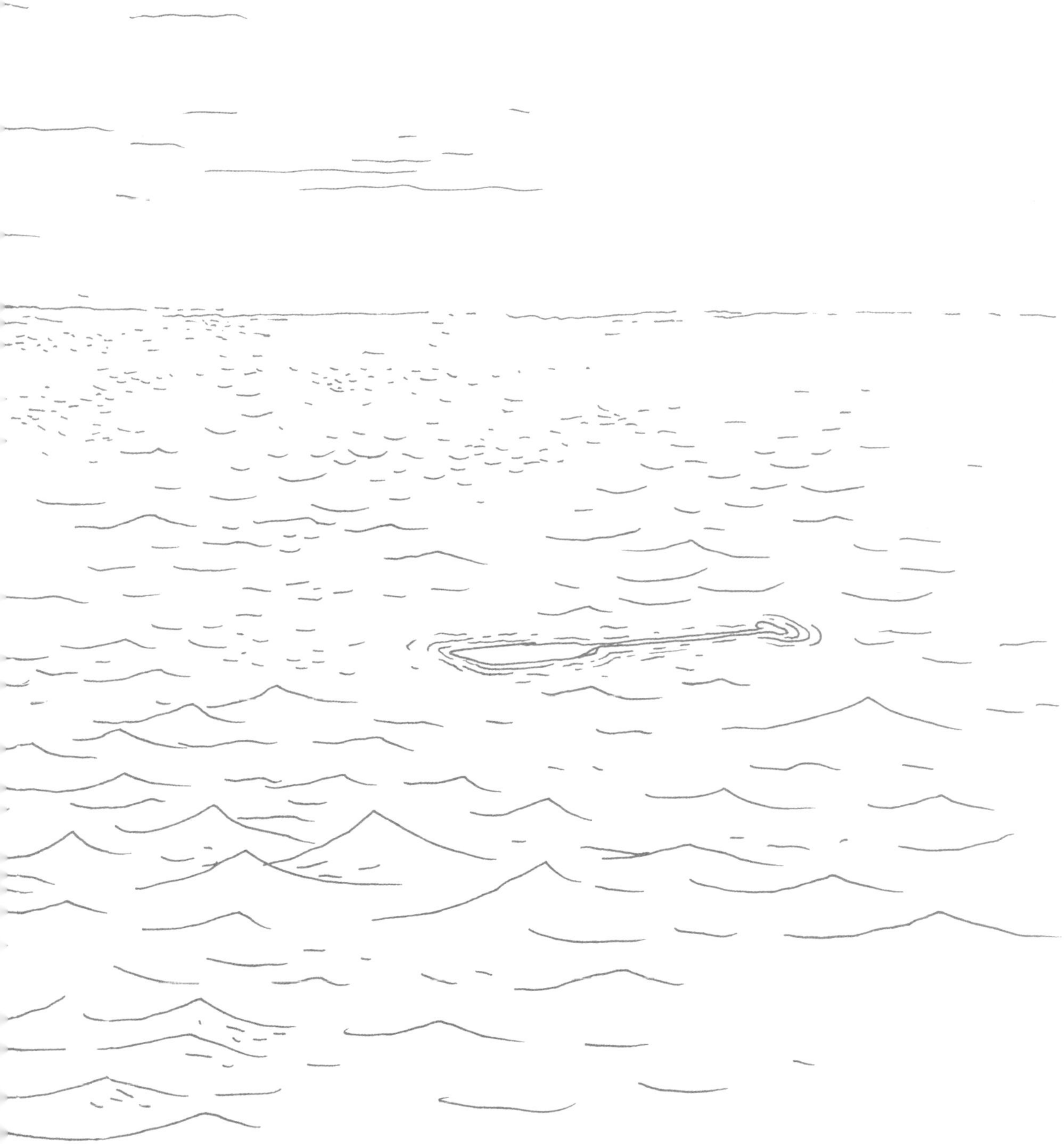

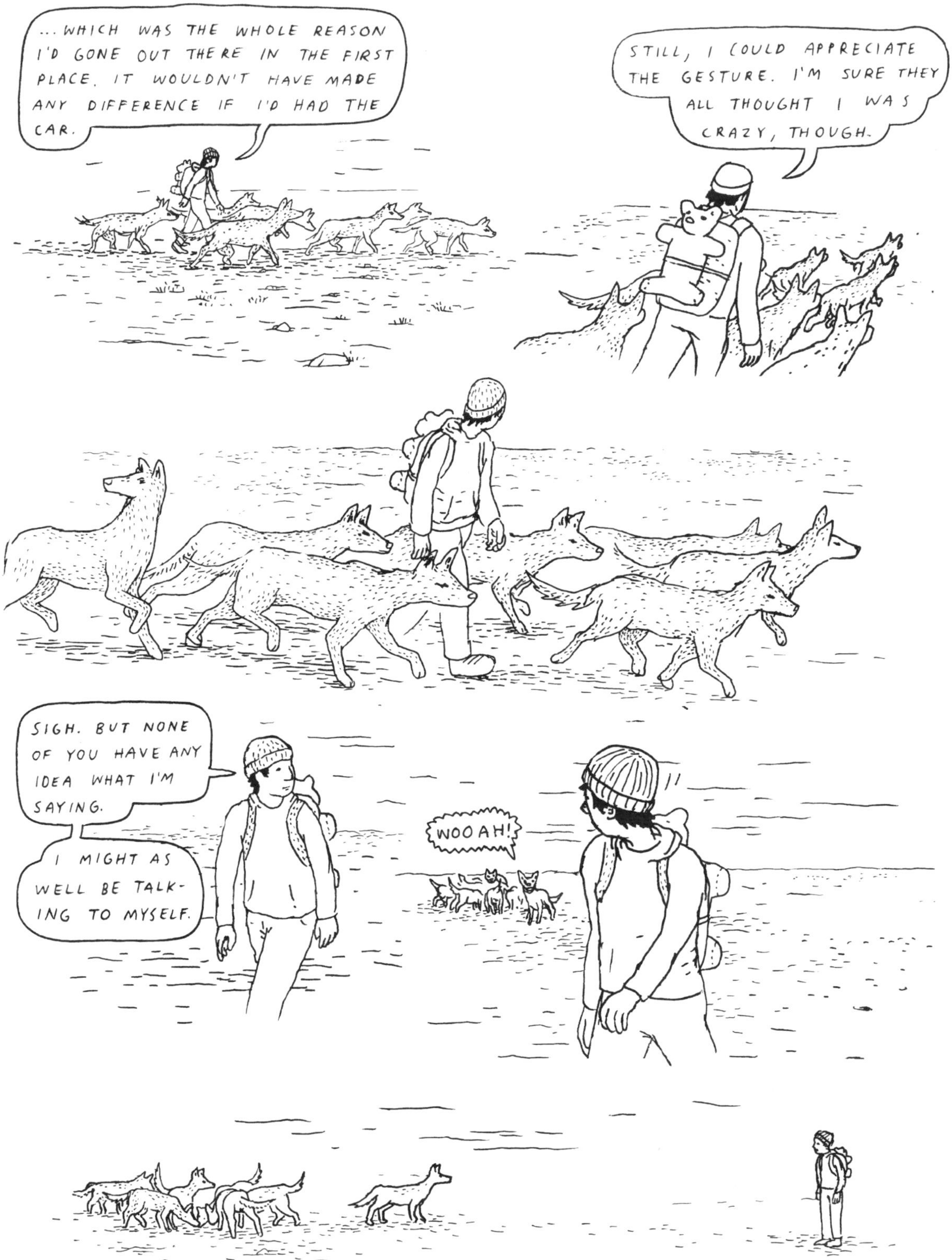
...WHICH WAS THE WHOLE REASON I'D GONE OUT THERE IN THE FIRST PLACE. IT WOULDN'T HAVE MADE ANY DIFFERENCE IF I'D HAD THE CAR.
STILL, I COULD APPRECIATE THE GESTURE. I'M SURE THEY ALL THOUGHT I WAS CRAZY, THOUGH.
SIGH. BUT NONE OF YOU HAVE ANY IDEA WHAT I'M SAYING.
I MIGHT AS WELL BE TALKING TO MYSELF.
WOOAH!

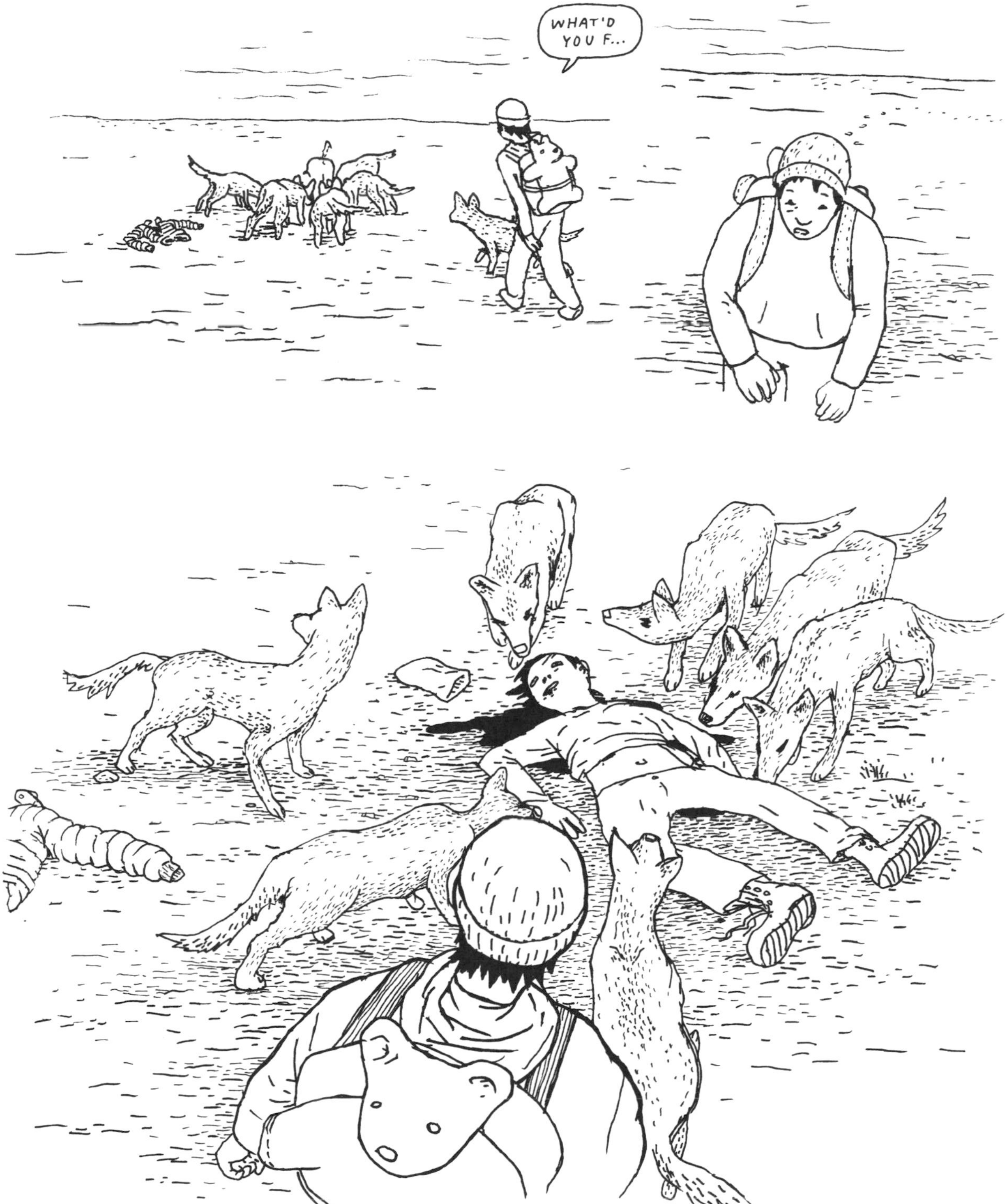
WHAT'D YOU F...

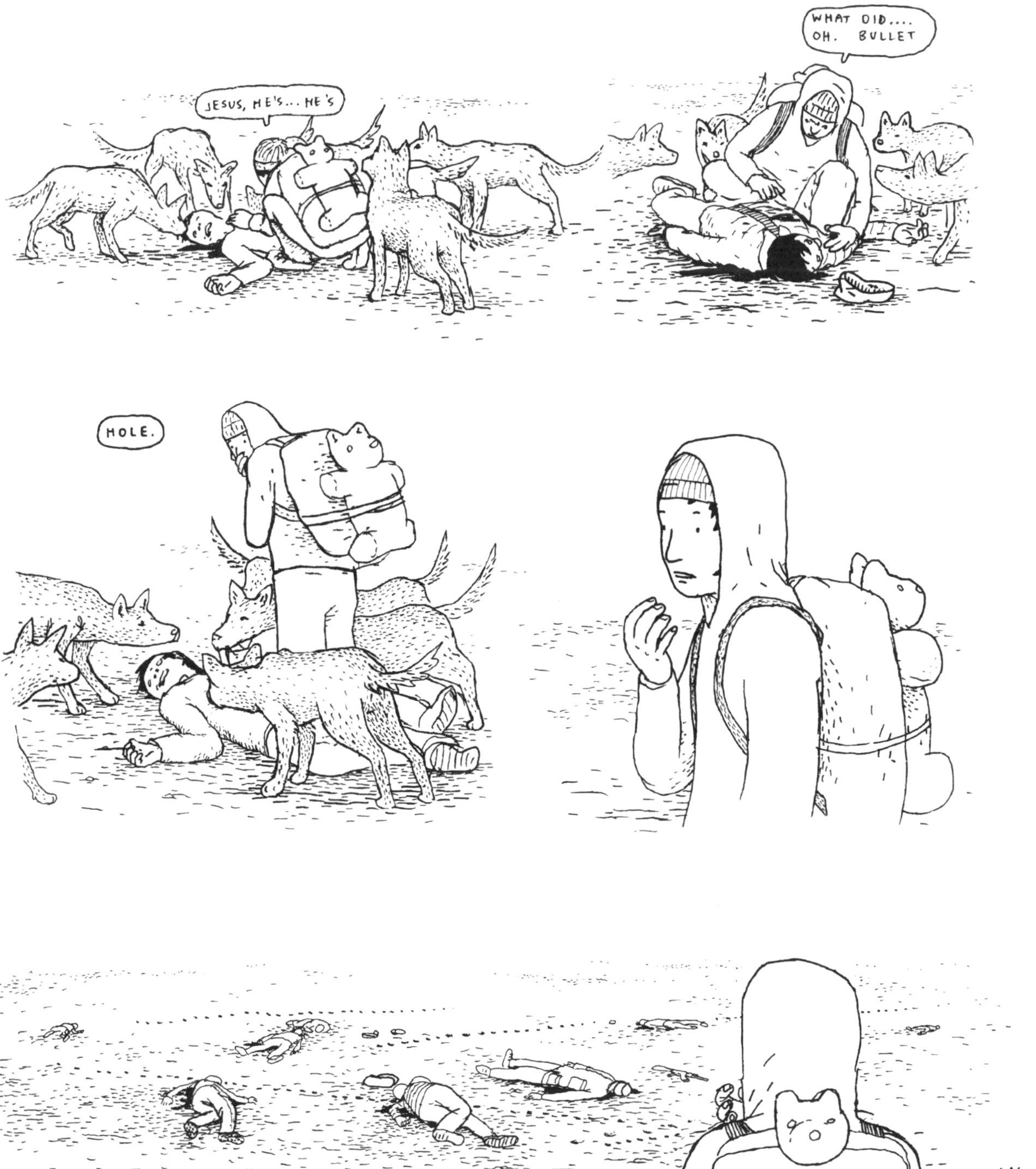
JESUS, HE'S... HE'S
WHAT DID.... OH. BULLET
HOLE.
CHK
CHK
CHC
KK

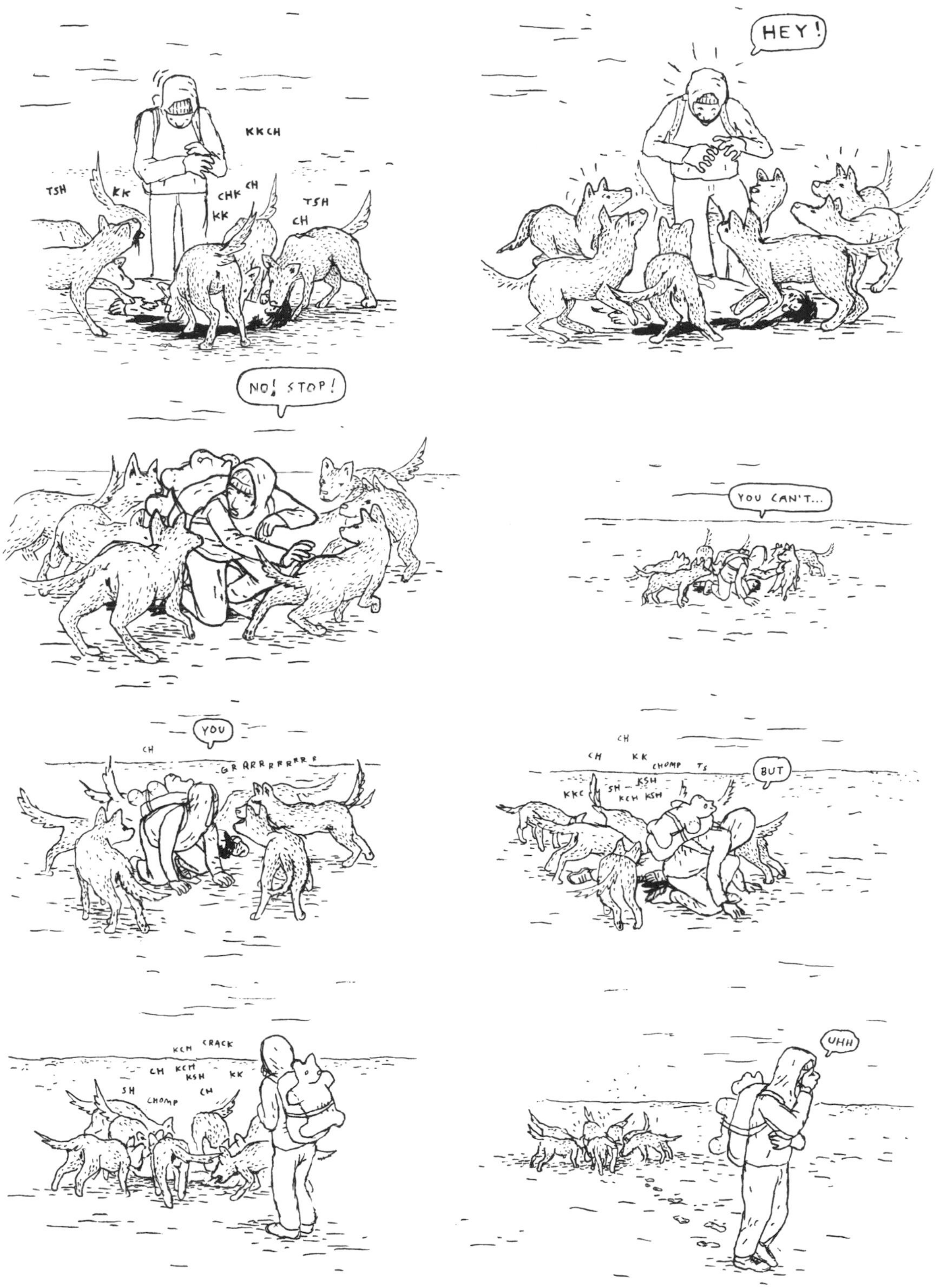
KKCH
TSH
KK
CHK
CH
KK
TSH
CH
HEY!
NO! STOP!
YOU CAN'T...
YOU
CH
GRARRRRRRRR
CH
CH
KK
CHOMP
TS
BUT
KKC
SH
KSH
KCH KSH
KCH CRACK
CH KCH
KSH
KK
SH
CHOMP
CH
UHH

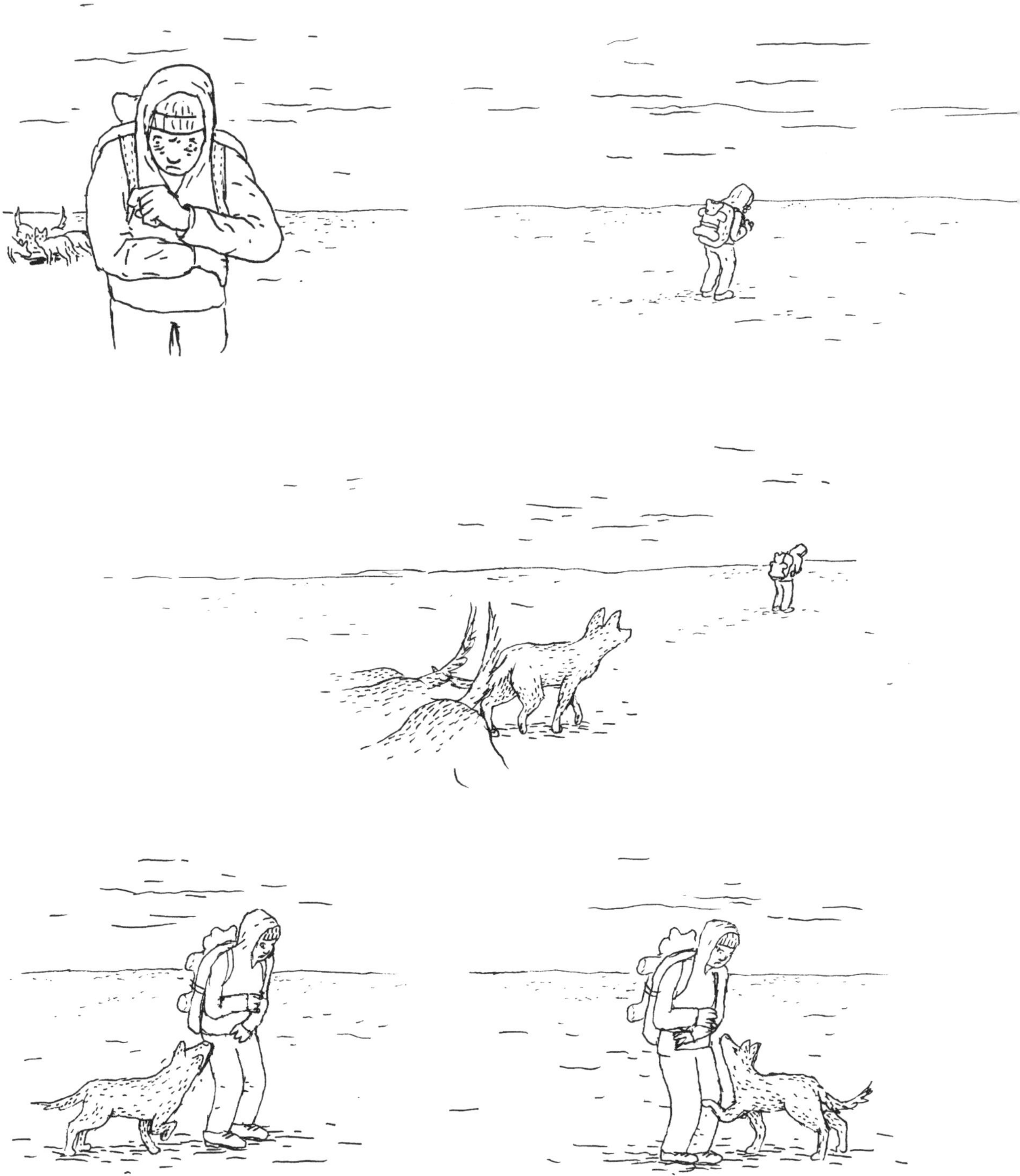

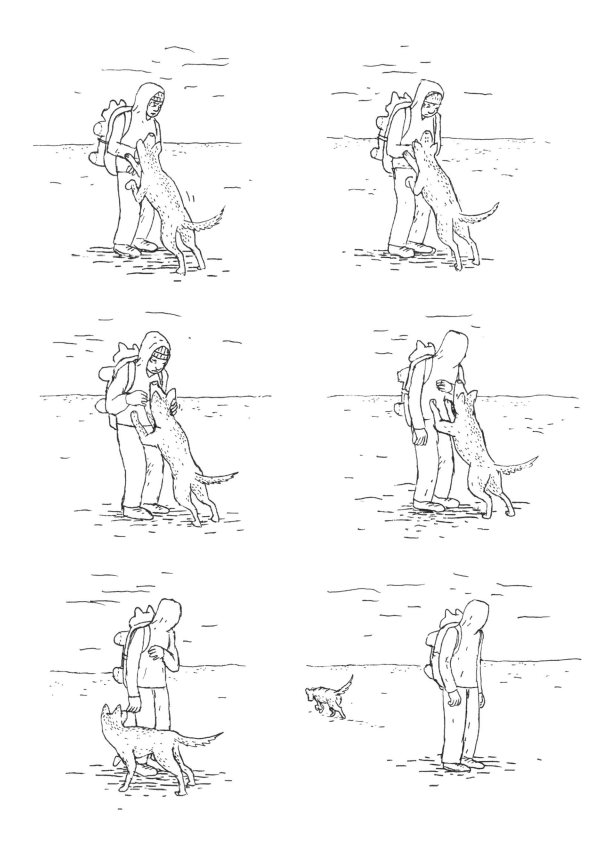

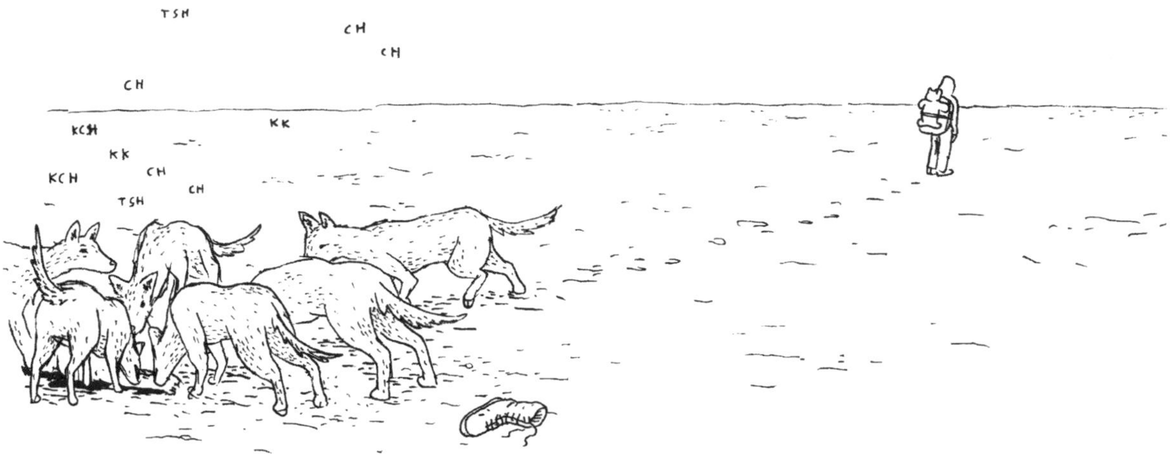
TSH
CH
CH
CH
KCH
KK
KK
KCH
CH
CH
TSH

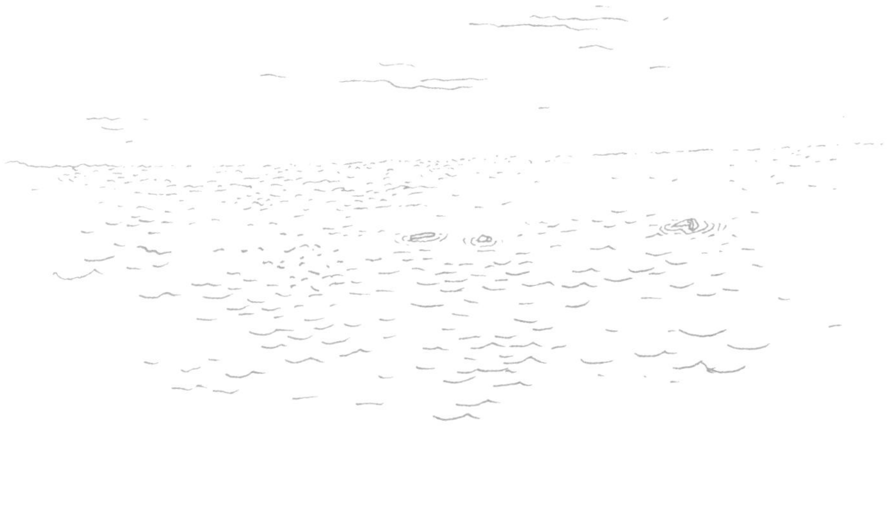

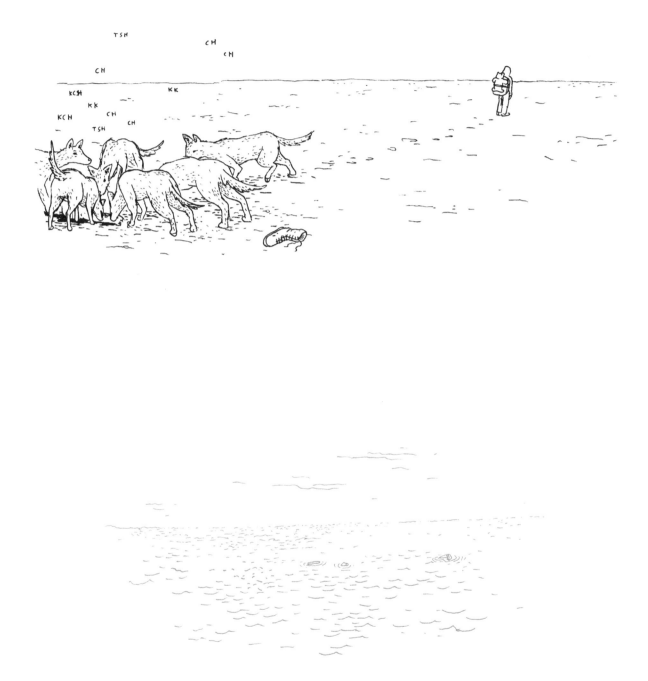

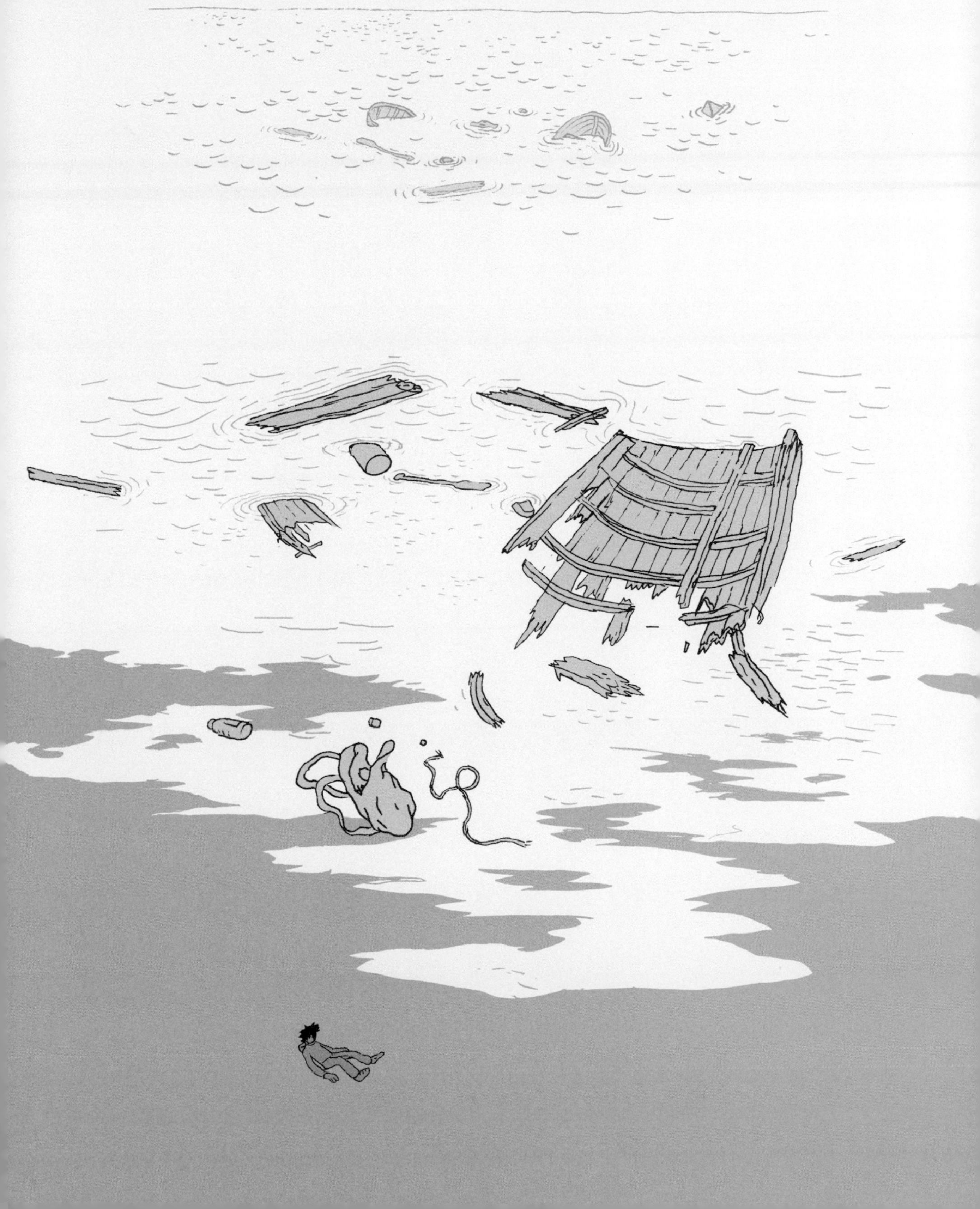

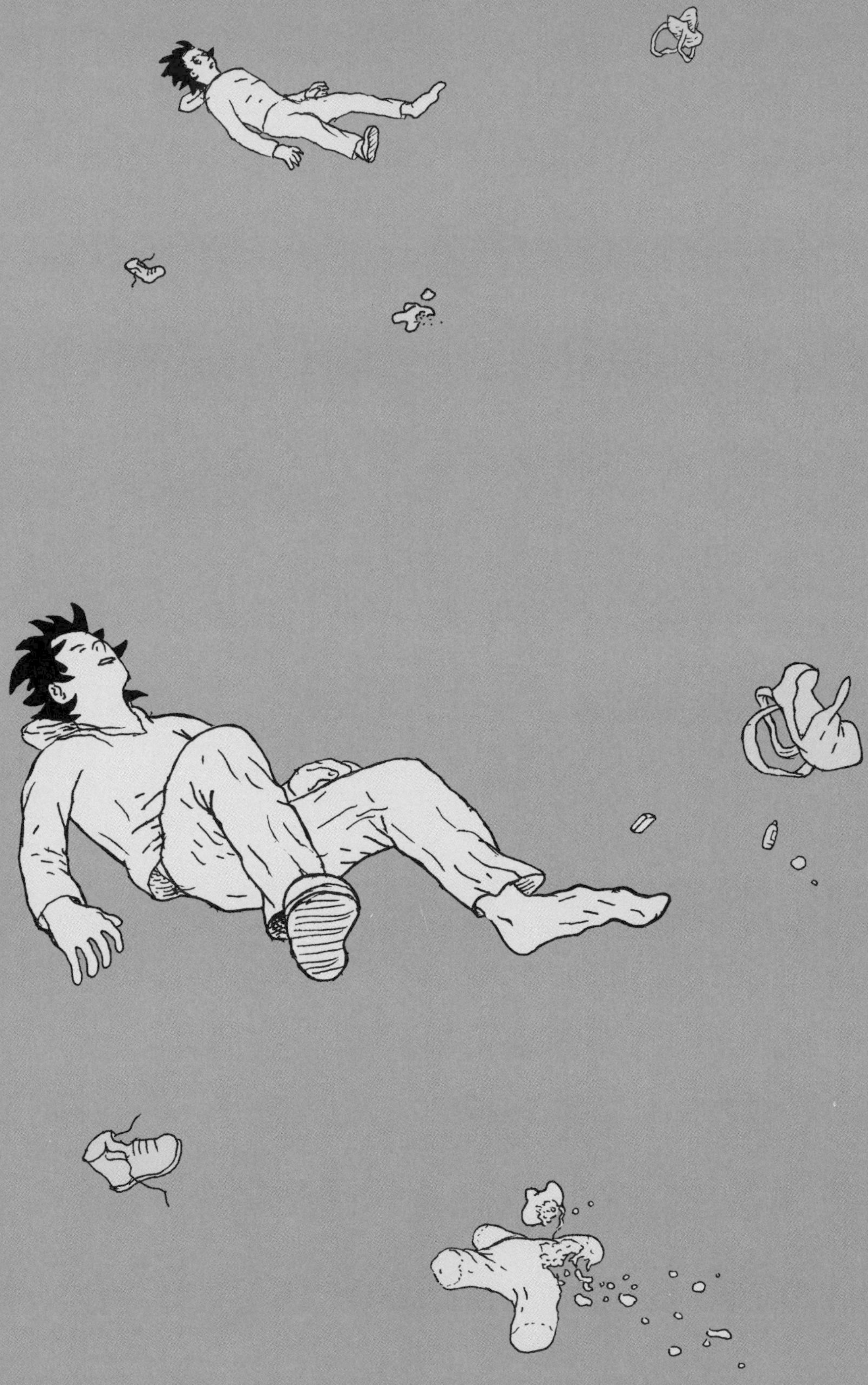

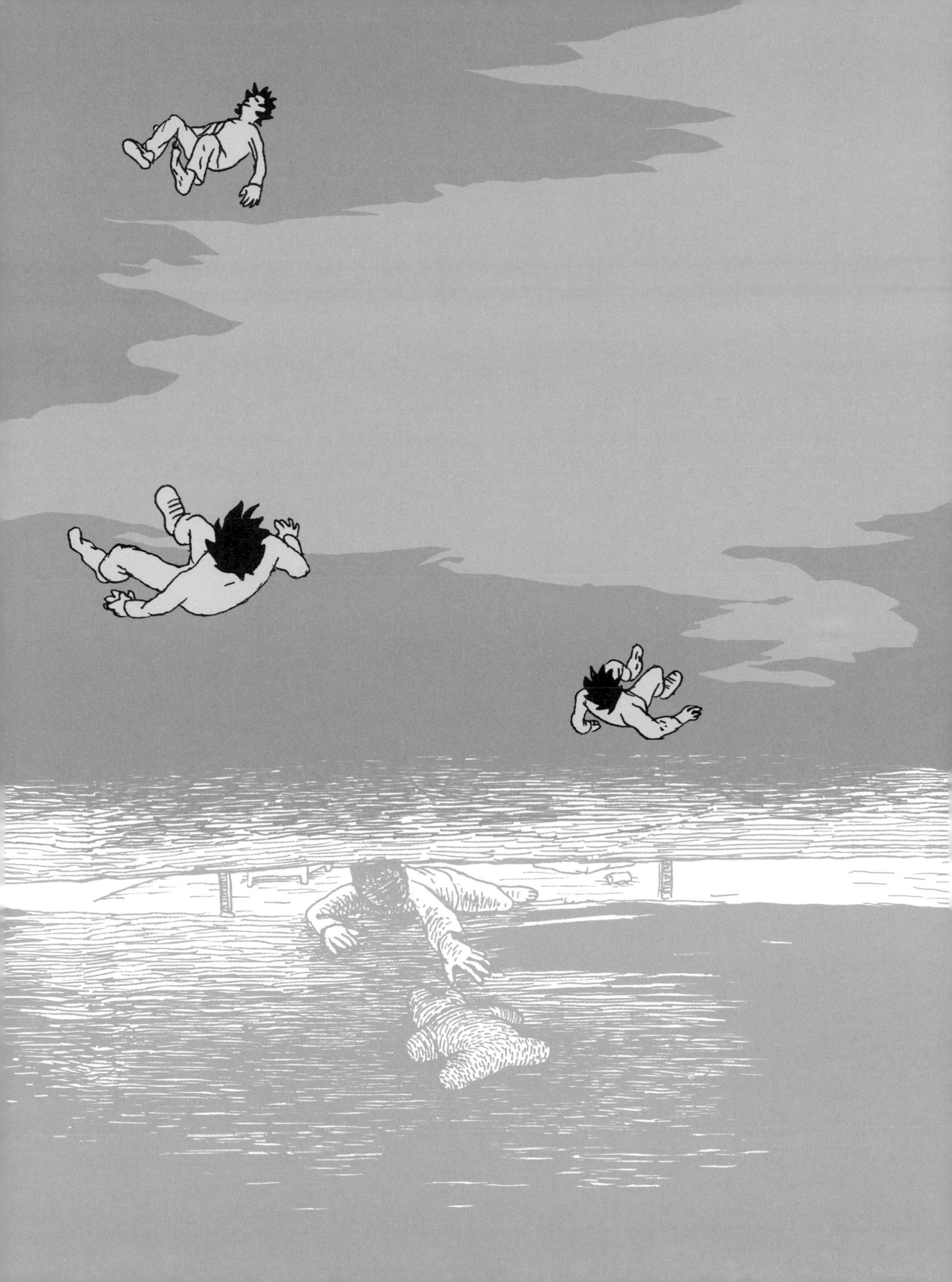

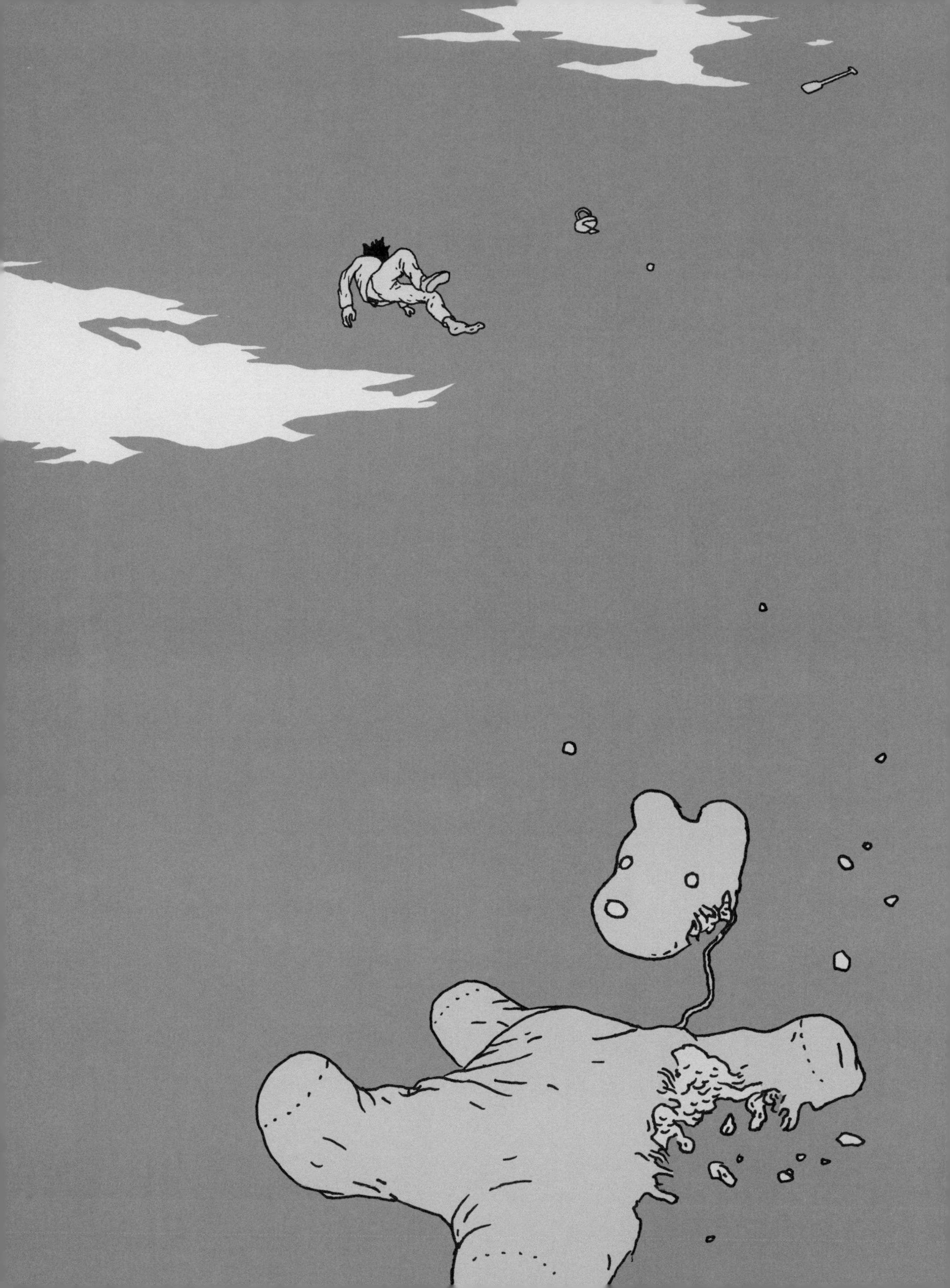

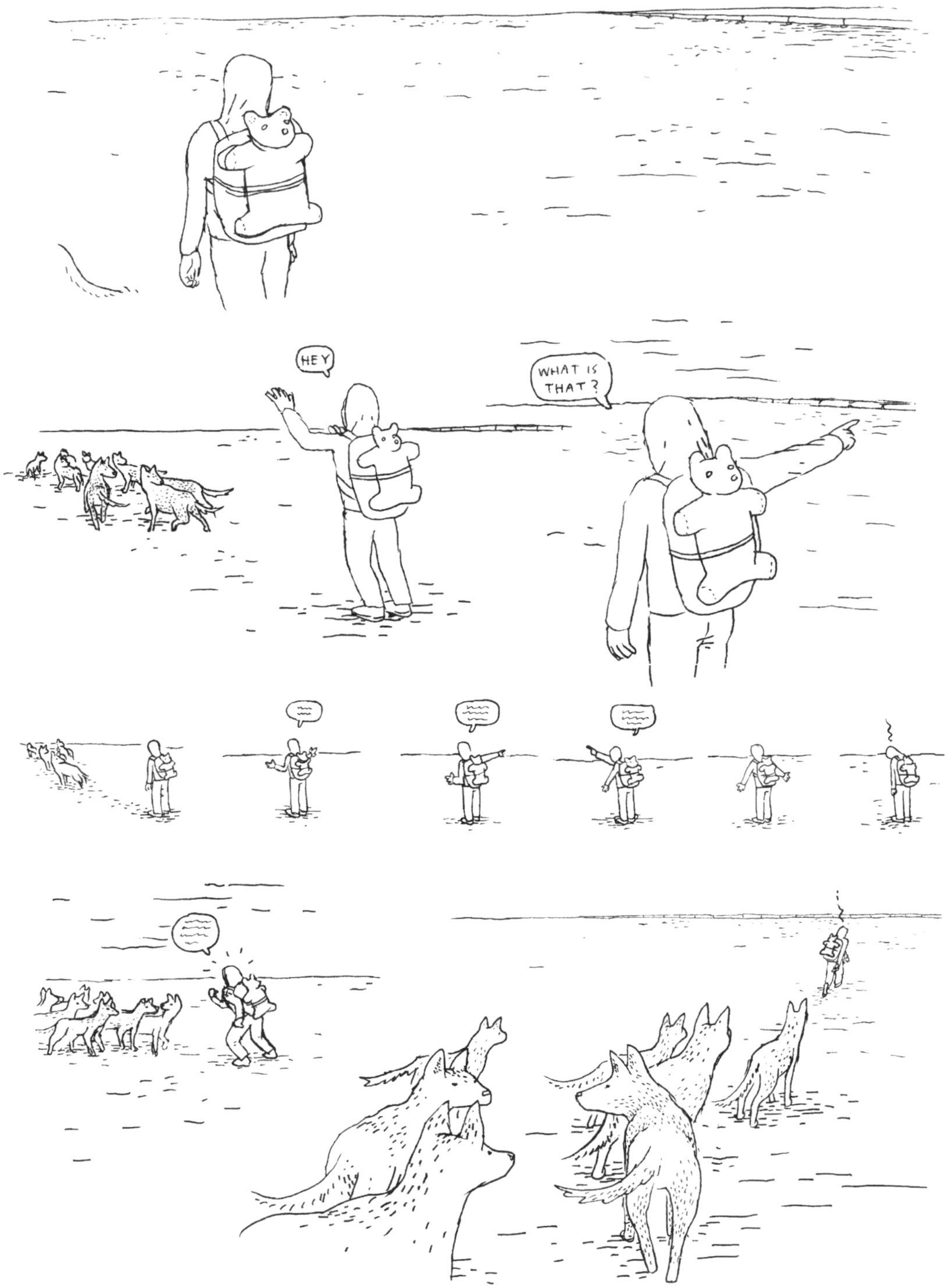
HEY
WHAT IS THAT?

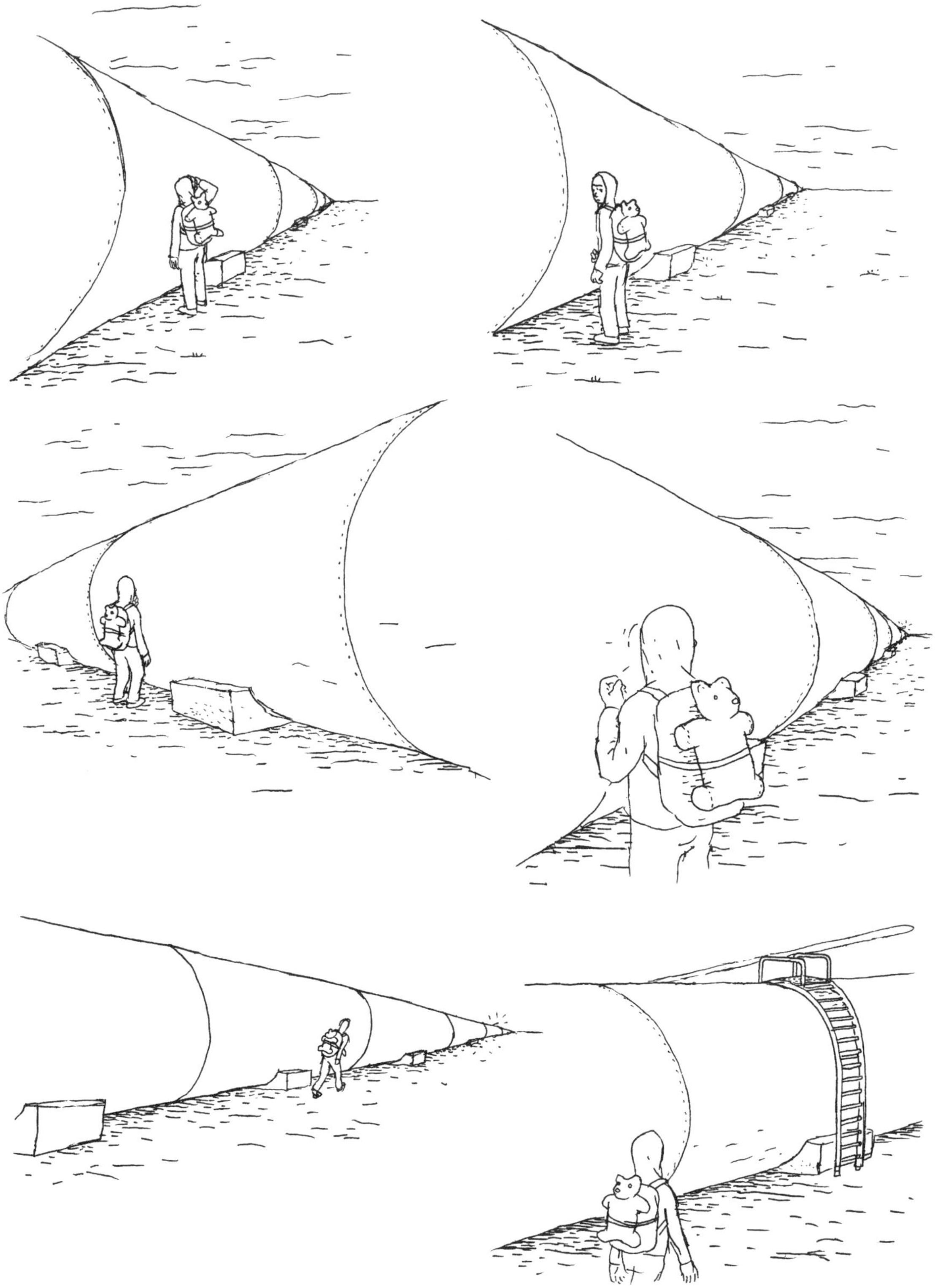

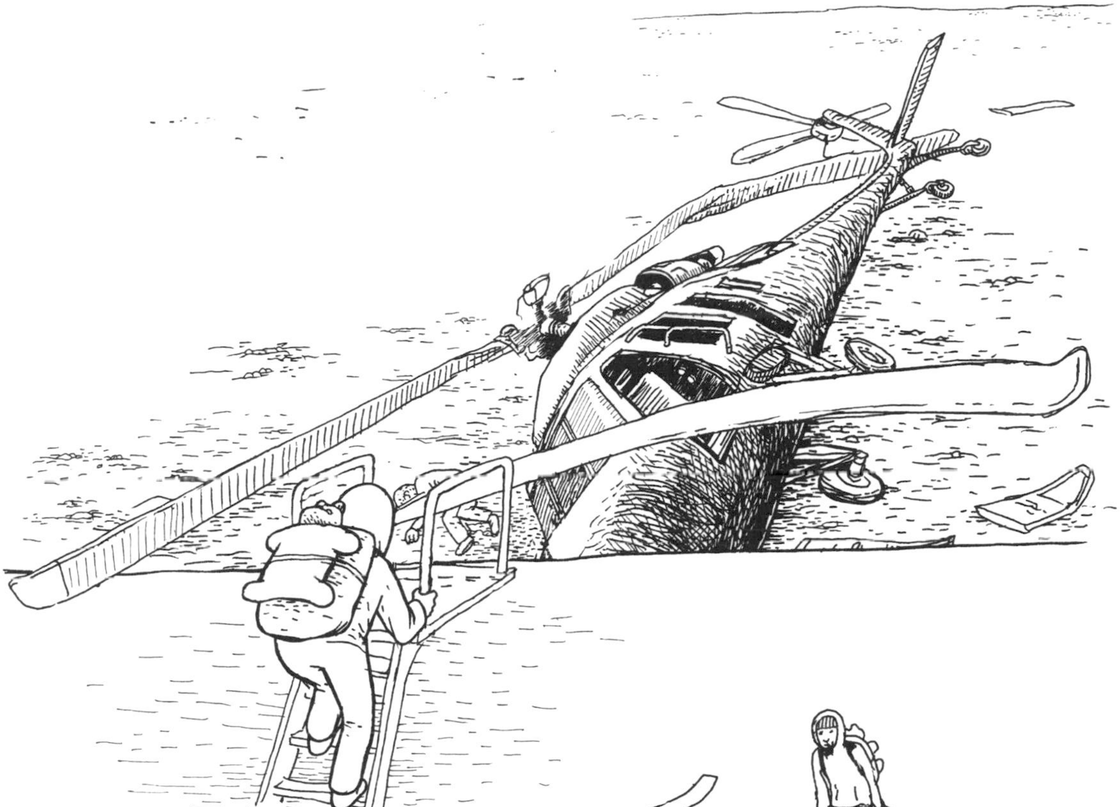

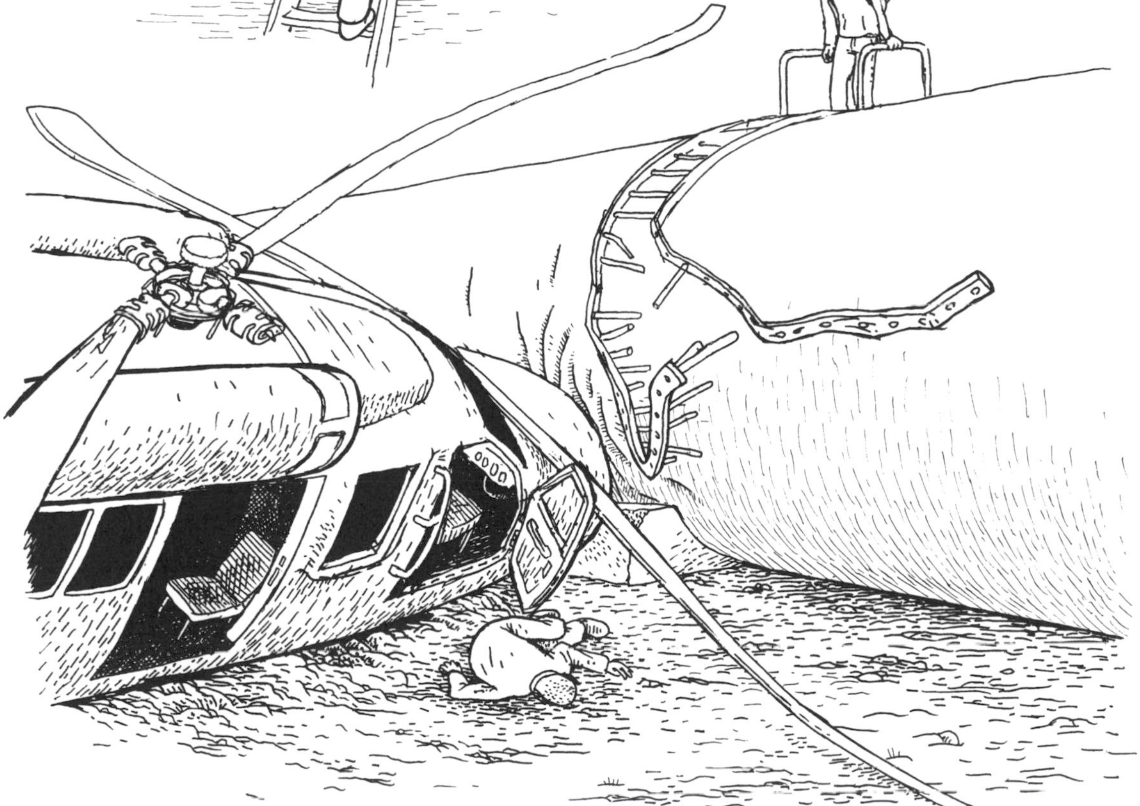

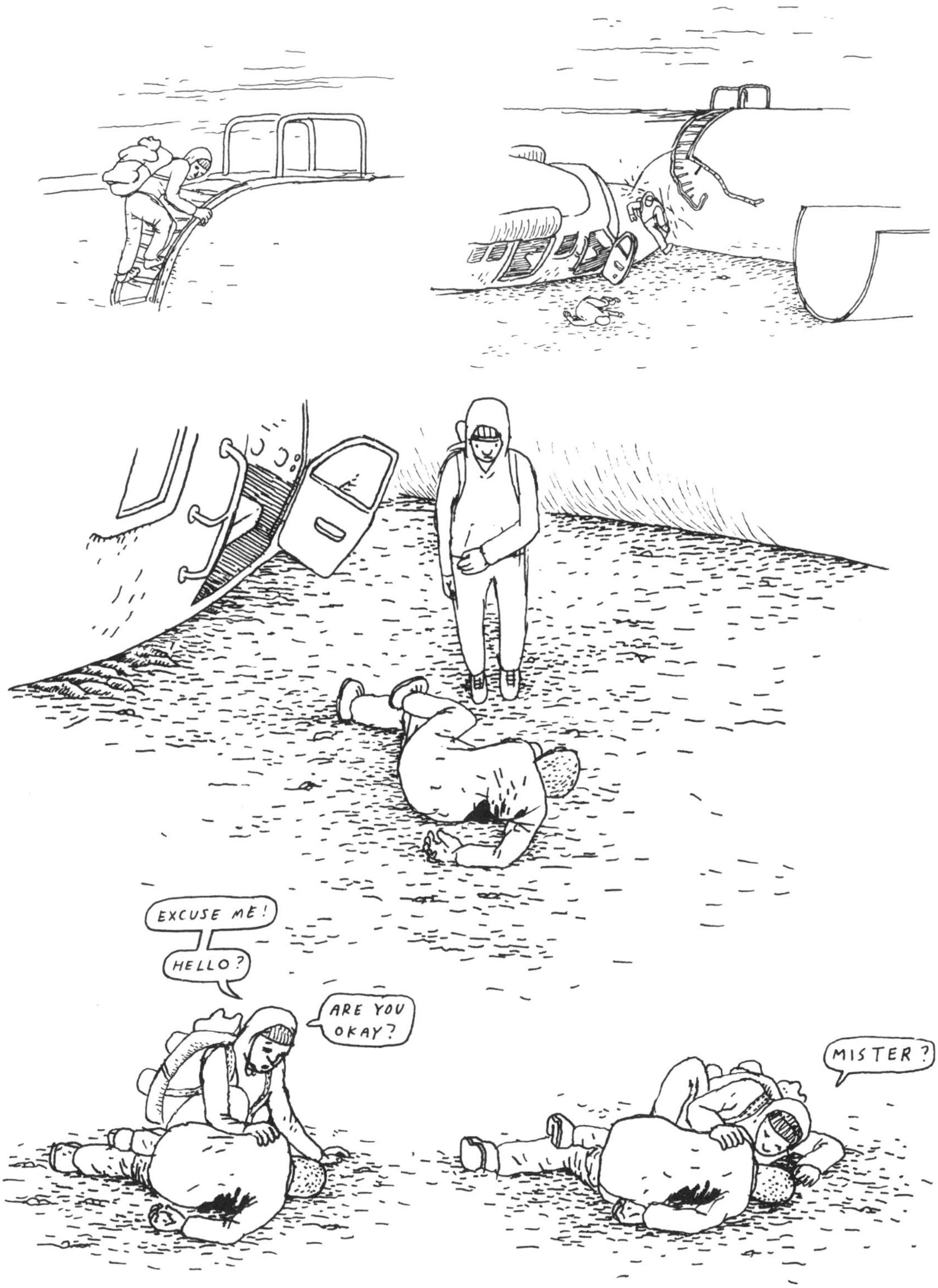
EXCUSE ME!
HELLO?
ARE YOU OKAY?
MISTER?

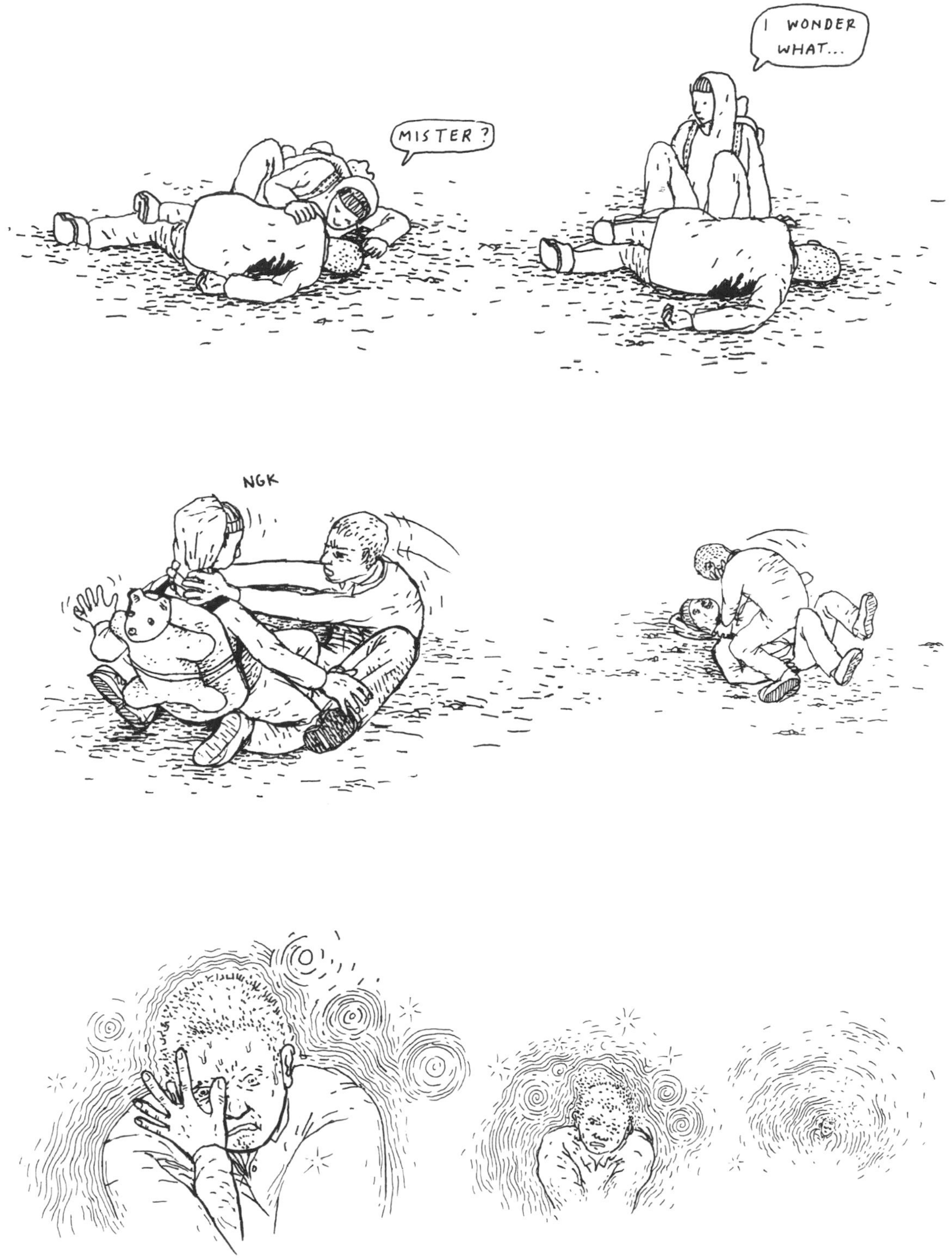
MISTER?
I WONDER WHAT...
NGK

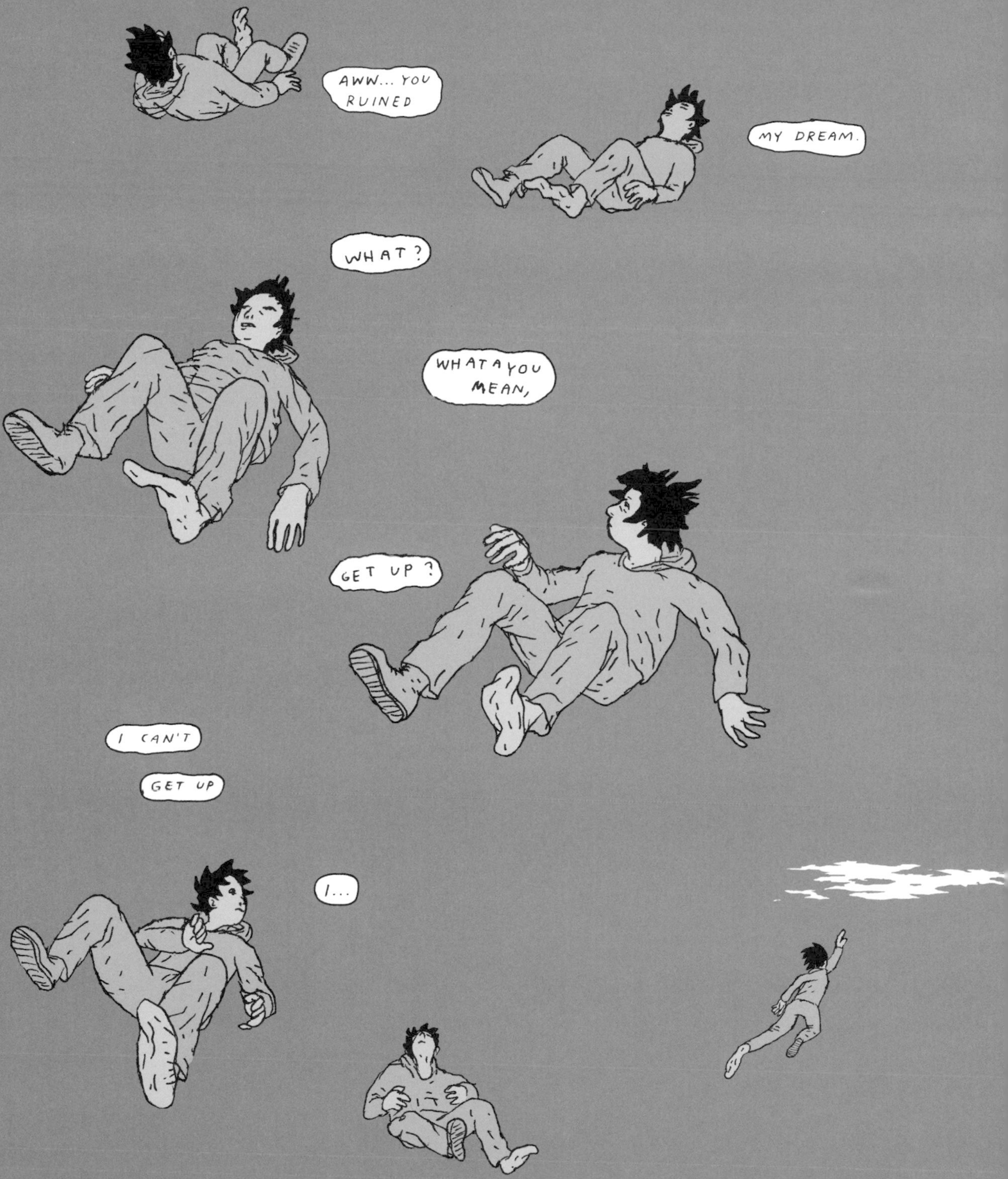
AWW... YOU RUINED
MY DREAM.
WHAT?
WHATAYOU MEAN,
GET UP?
I CAN'T
GET UP
I...

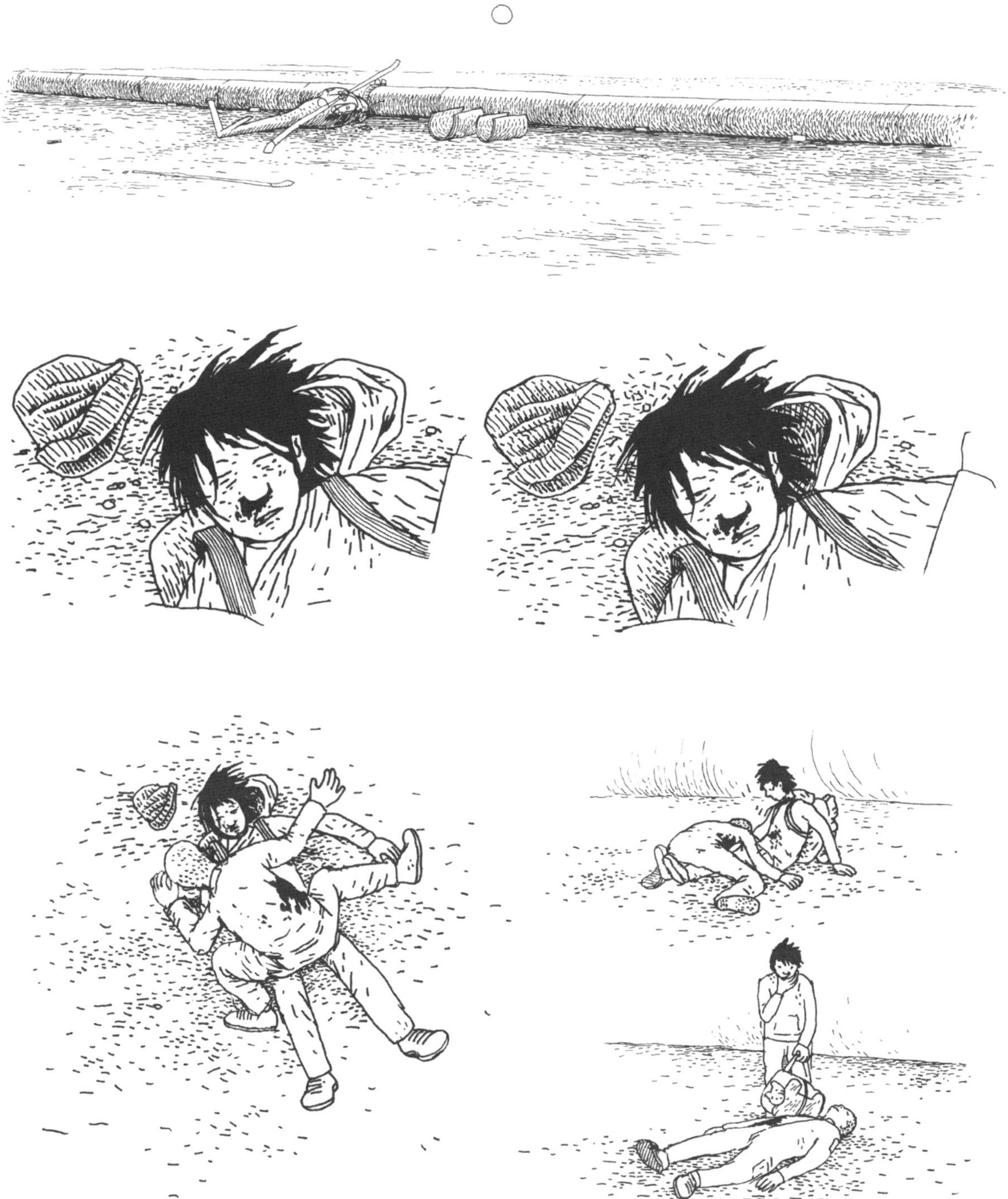

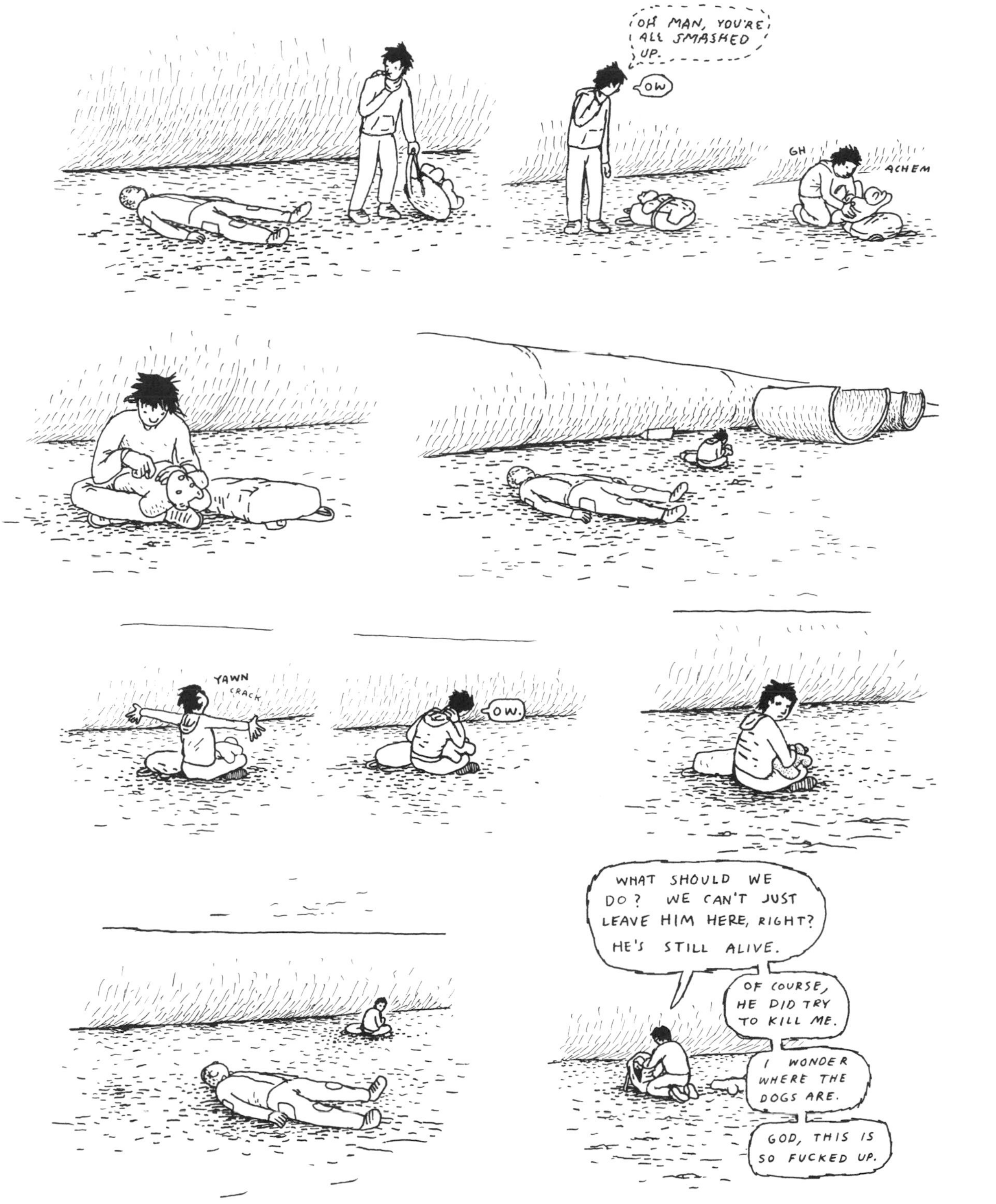
OH MAN, YOU'RE ALL SMASHED UP.
OW
GH
ACHEM
YAWN
CRACK
OW.
WHAT SHOULD WE DO? WE CAN'T JUST LEAVE HIM HERE, RIGHT? HE'S STILL ALIVE.
OF COURSE, HE DID TRY TO KILL ME.
I WONDER WHERE THE DOGS ARE.
GOD, THIS IS SO FUCKED UP.

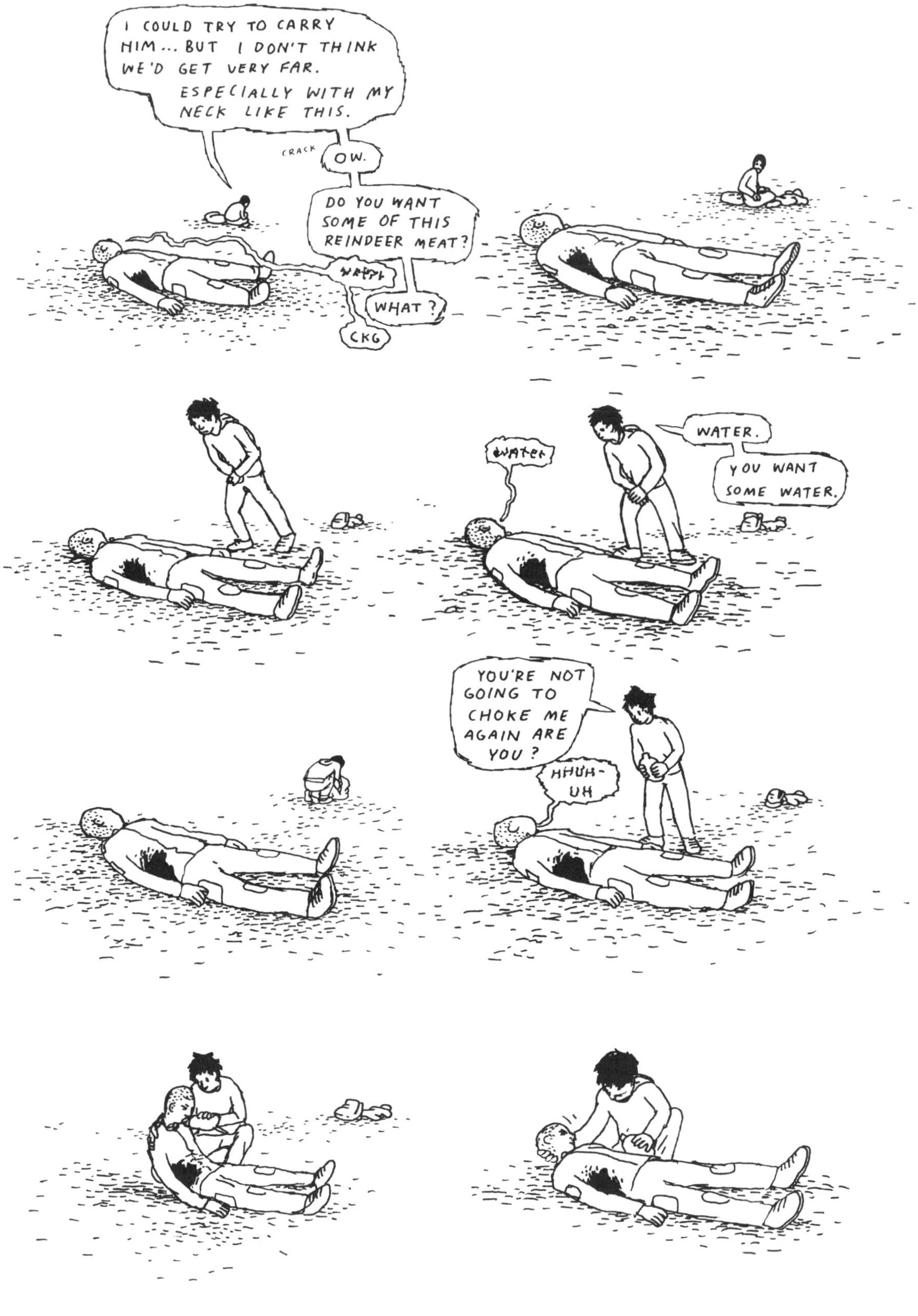
I COULD TRY TO CARRY HIM... BUT I DON'T THINK WE'D GET VERY FAR.
ESPECIALLY WITH MY NECK LIKE THIS.
CRACK
OW.
DO YOU WANT SOME OF THIS REINDEER MEAT?
WHAT?
CKG
WATER.
YOU WANT SOME WATER.
YOU'RE NOT GOING TO CHOKE ME AGAIN ARE YOU?
HHUH-UH

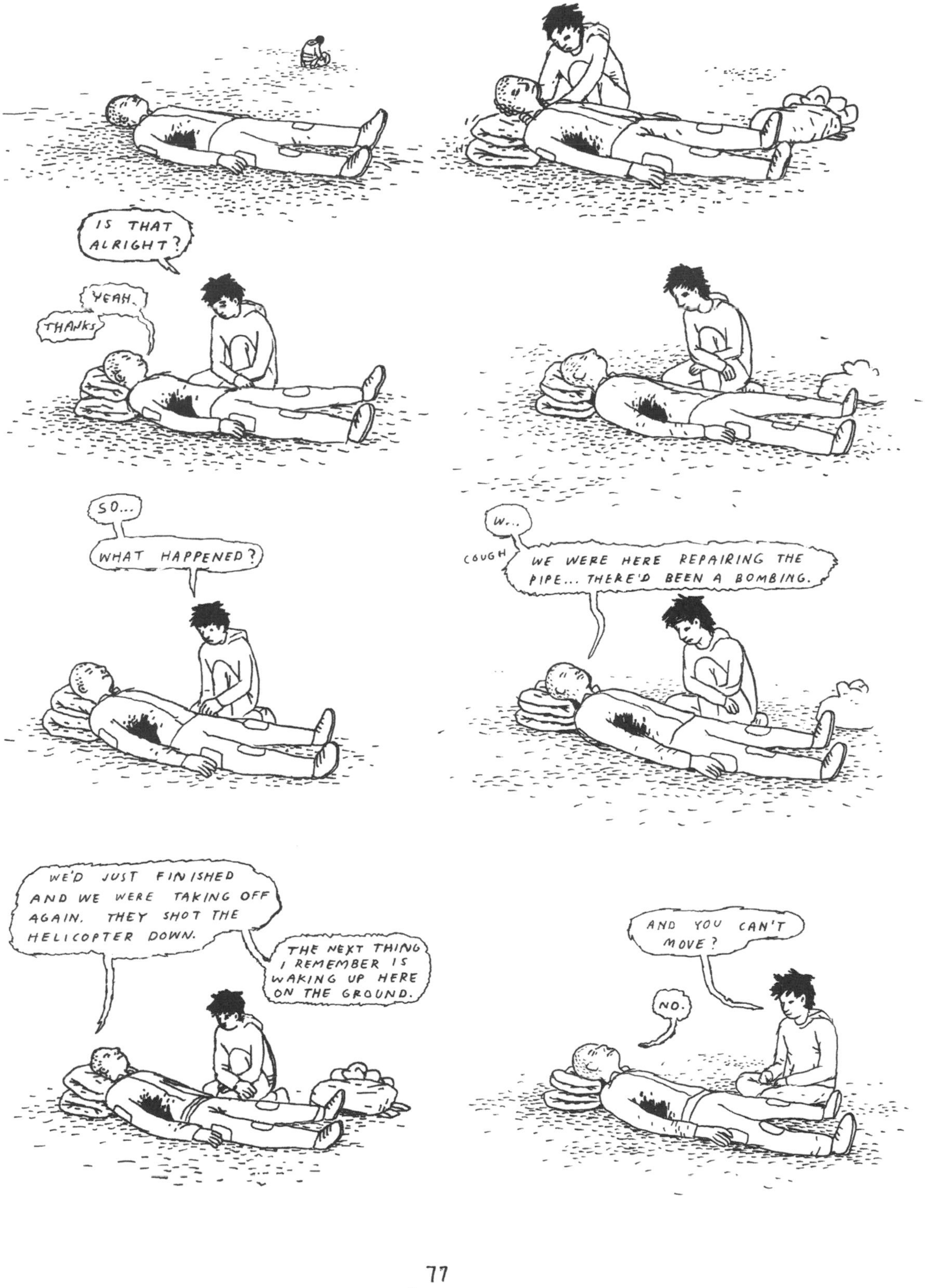
IS THAT ALRIGHT?
YEAH.
THANKS
SO...
WHAT HAPPENED?
W...
COUGH
WE WERE HERE REPAIRING THE PIPE... THERE'D BEEN A BOMBING.
WE'D JUST FINISHED AND WE WERE TAKING OFF AGAIN. THEY SHOT THE HELICOPTER DOWN.
THE NEXT THING I REMEMBER IS WAKING UP HERE ON THE GROUND.
AND YOU CAN'T MOVE?
NO.

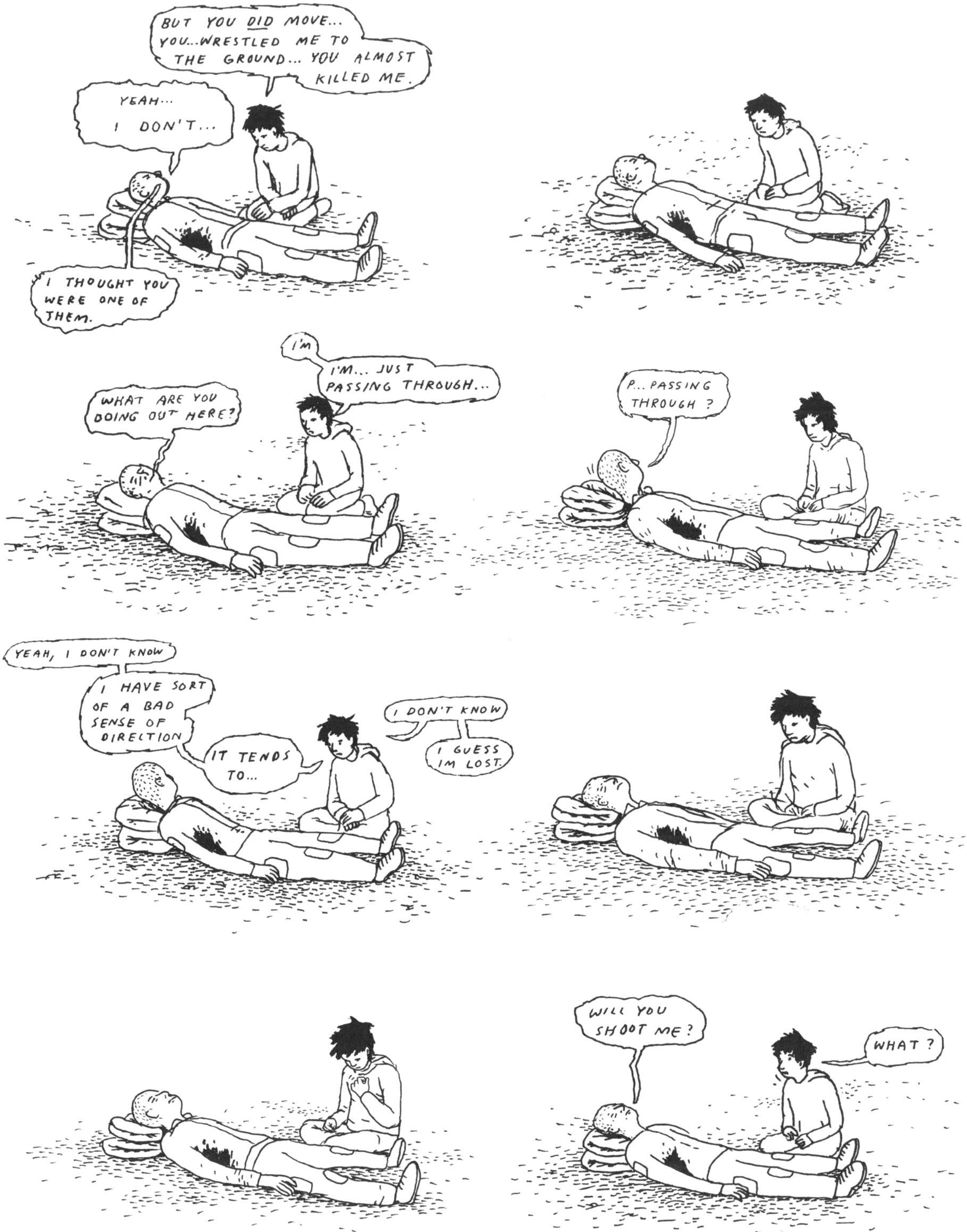
BUT YOU DID MOVE... YOU...WRESTLED ME TO THE GROUND... YOU ALMOST KILLED ME.
YEAH... I DON'T...
I THOUGHT YOU WERE ONE OF THEM.
WHAT ARE YOU DOING OUT HERE?
I'M
I'M... JUST PASSING THROUGH...
P... PASSING THROUGH?
YEAH, I DON'T KNOW
I HAVE SORT OF A BAD SENSE OF DIRECTION
IT TENDS TO...
I DON'T KNOW
I GUESS IM LOST.
WILL YOU SHOOT ME?
WHAT?

I
I... DON'T KNOW IF I...
WITH WHAT?
THERE'S A SIDEARM UNDER EACH SEAT IN THE HELICOPTER
ARE... ARE YOU...?
YES. I'M SURE.
I'VE BEEN THINKING ABOUT THIS FOR FOUR DAYS
PLEASE.

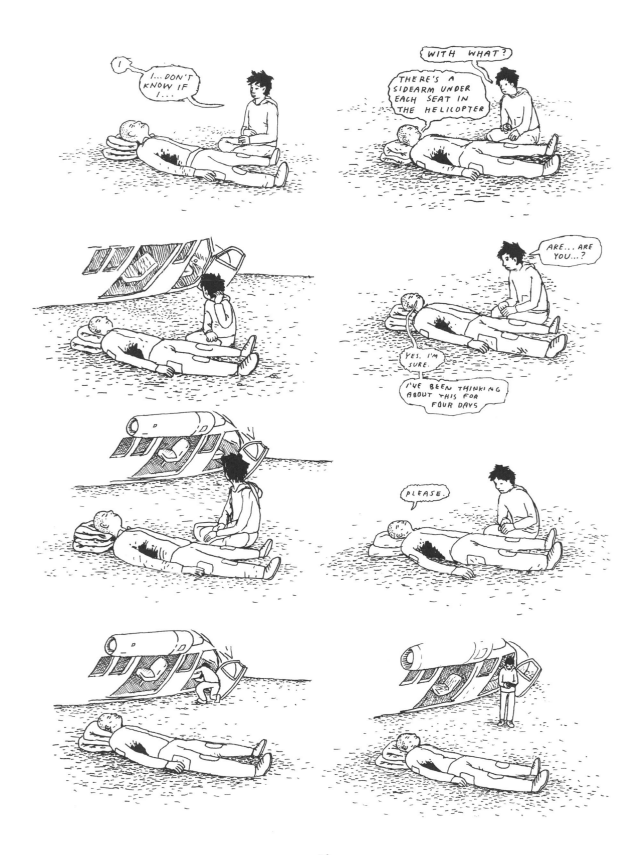

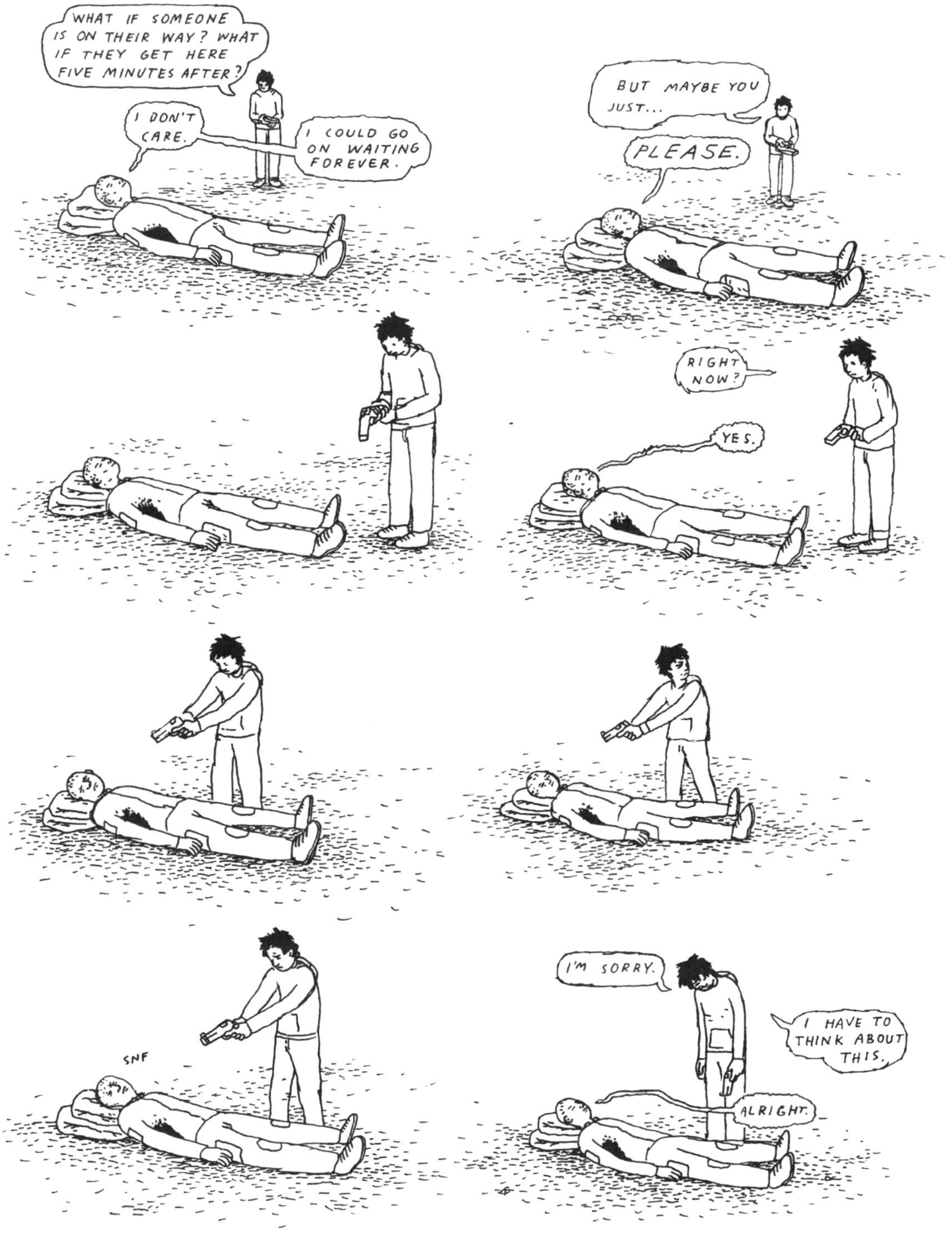
WHAT IF SOMEONE IS ON THEIR WAY? WHAT IF THEY GET HERE FIVE MINUTES AFTER?
I DON'T CARE.
I COULD GO ON WAITING FOREVER.
BUT MAYBE YOU JUST...
PLEASE.
RIGHT NOW?
YES.
SNF
I'M SORRY.
I HAVE TO THINK ABOUT THIS.
ALRIGHT.

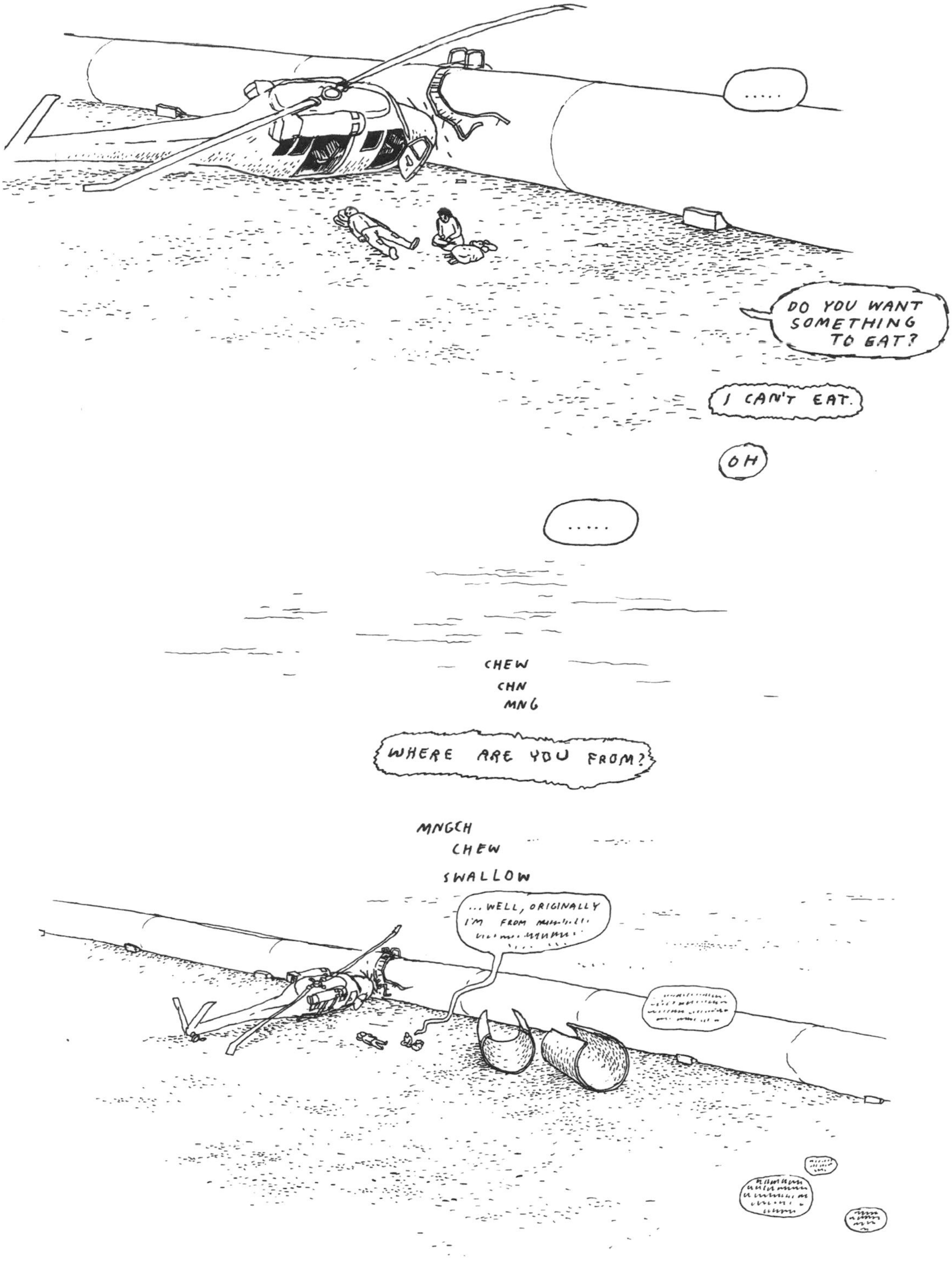
.....
DO YOU WANT SOMETHING TO EAT?
I CAN'T EAT.
OH
.....
CHEW
CHN
MNG
WHERE ARE YOU FROM?
MNGCH
CHEW
SWALLOW
...WELL, ORIGINALLY I'M FROM

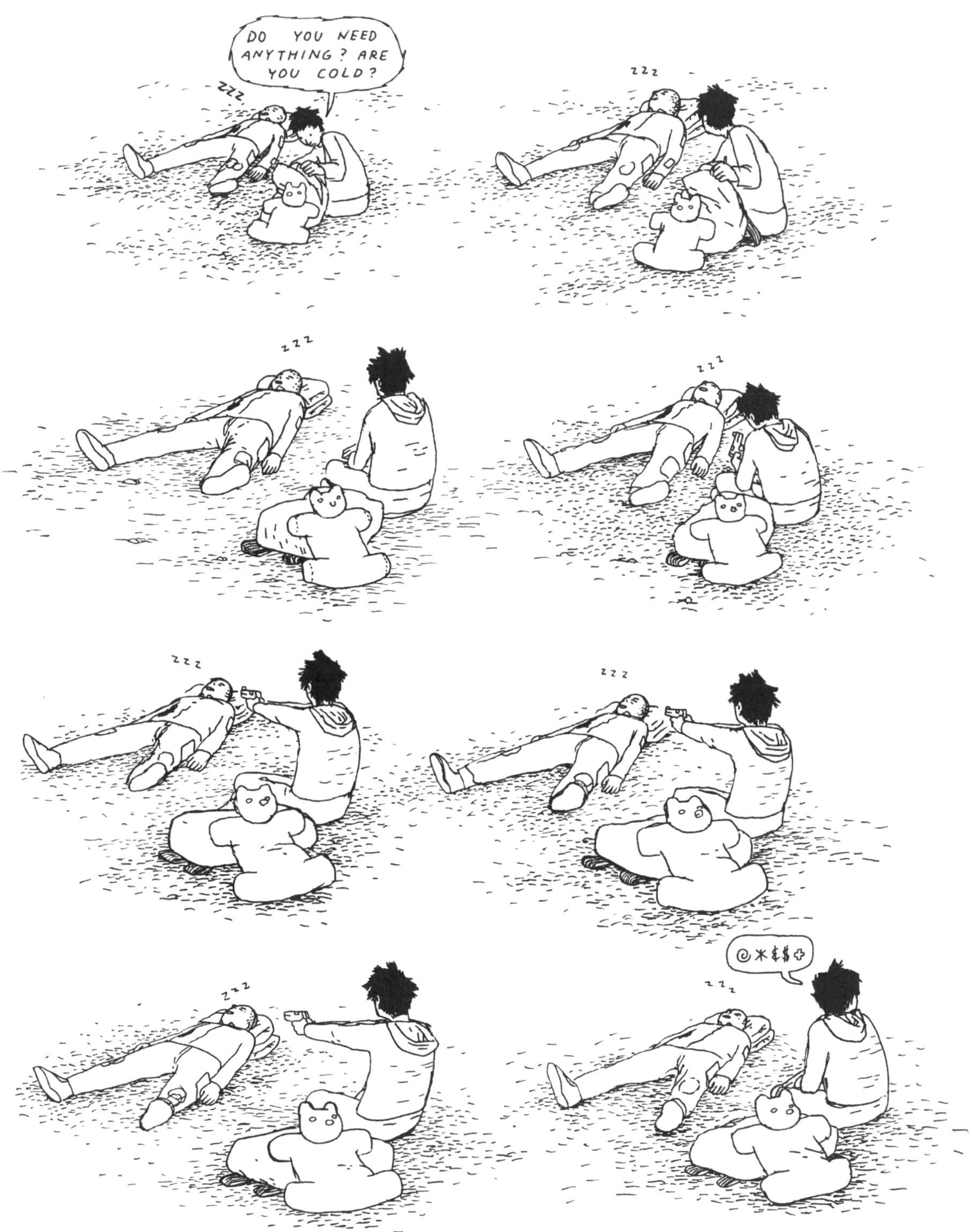
DO YOU NEED ANYTHING? ARE YOU COLD?

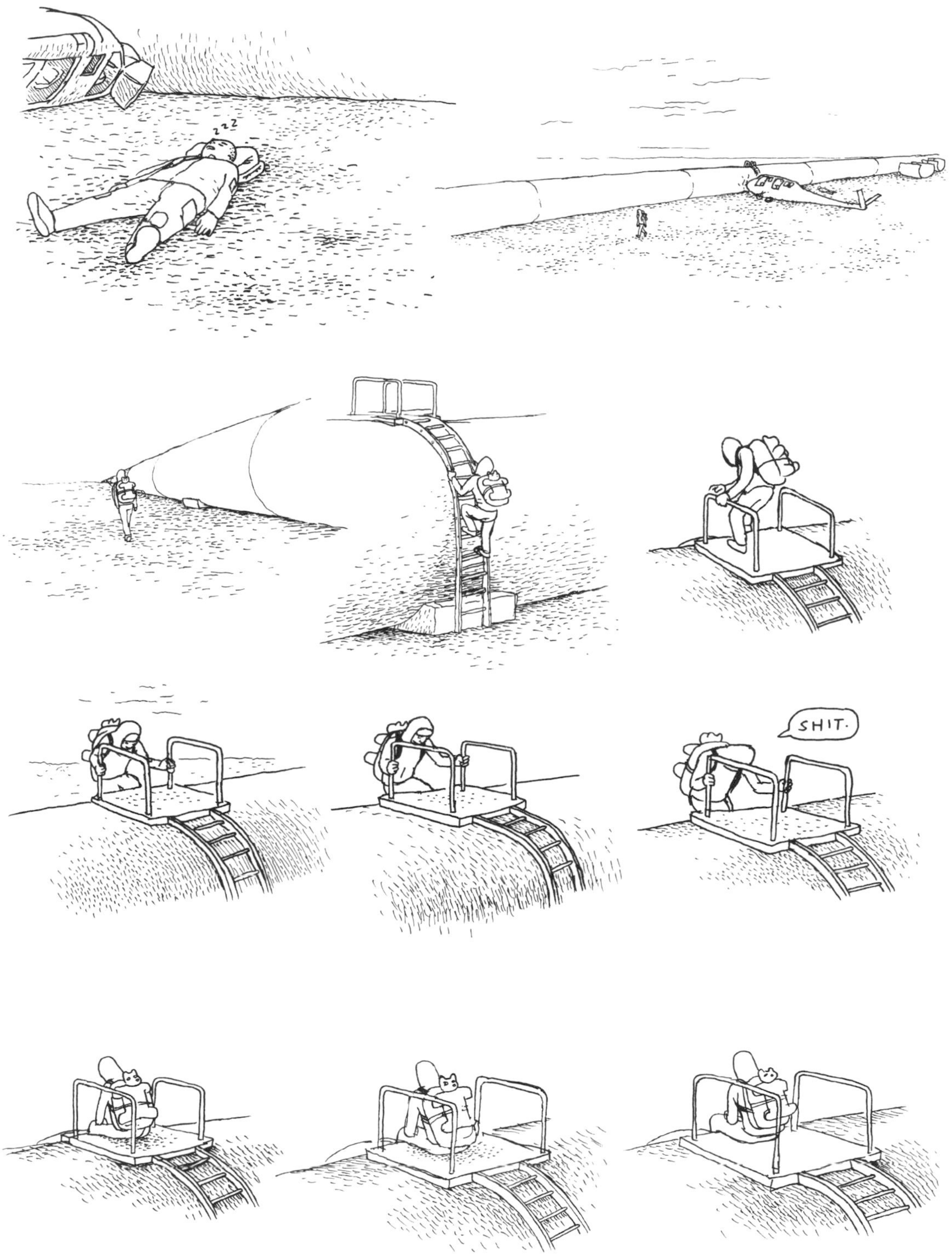
zzz
SHIT.

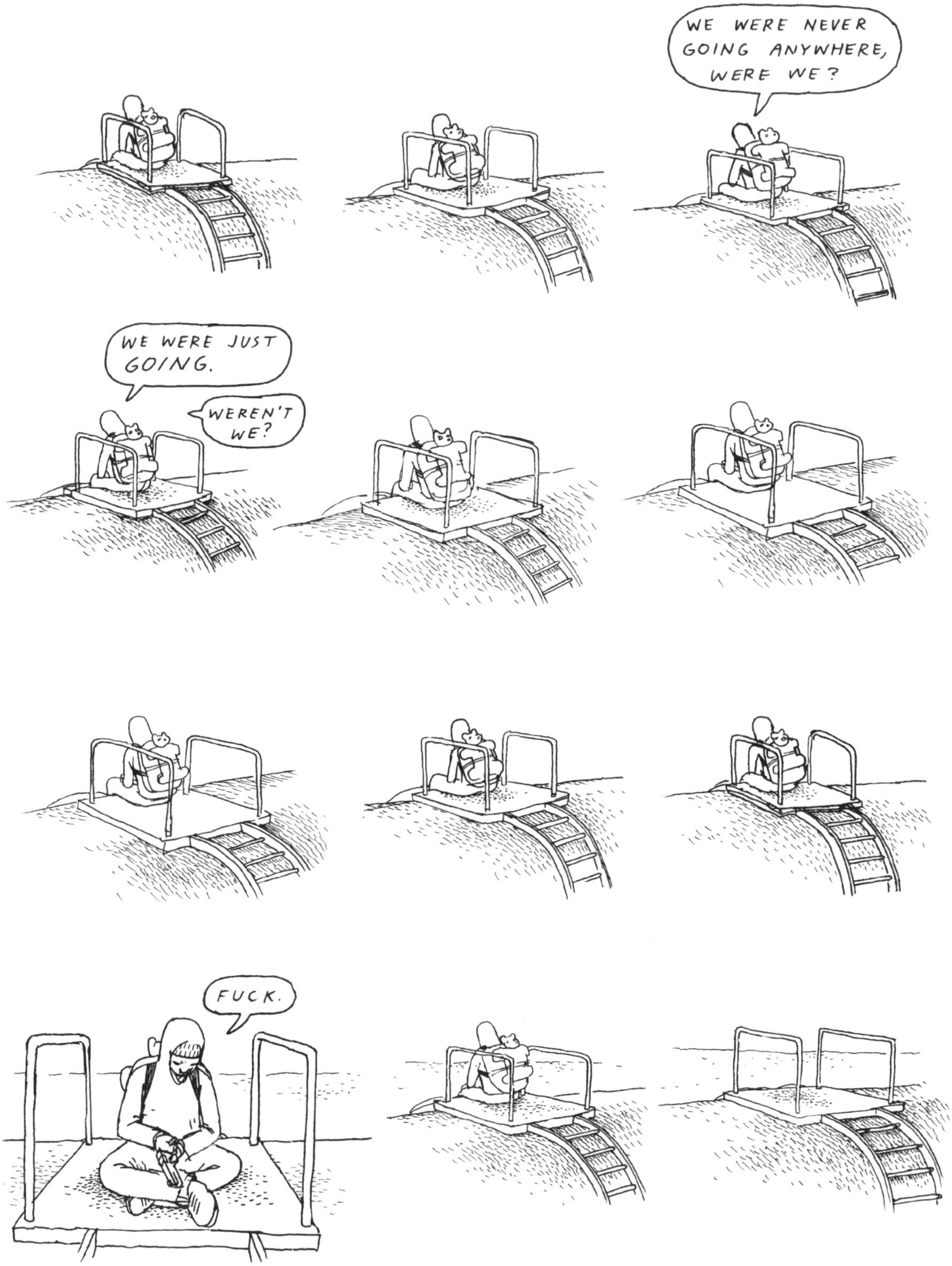
WE WERE NEVER GOING ANYWHERE, WERE WE?
WE WERE JUST GOING.
WEREN'T WE?
FUCK.

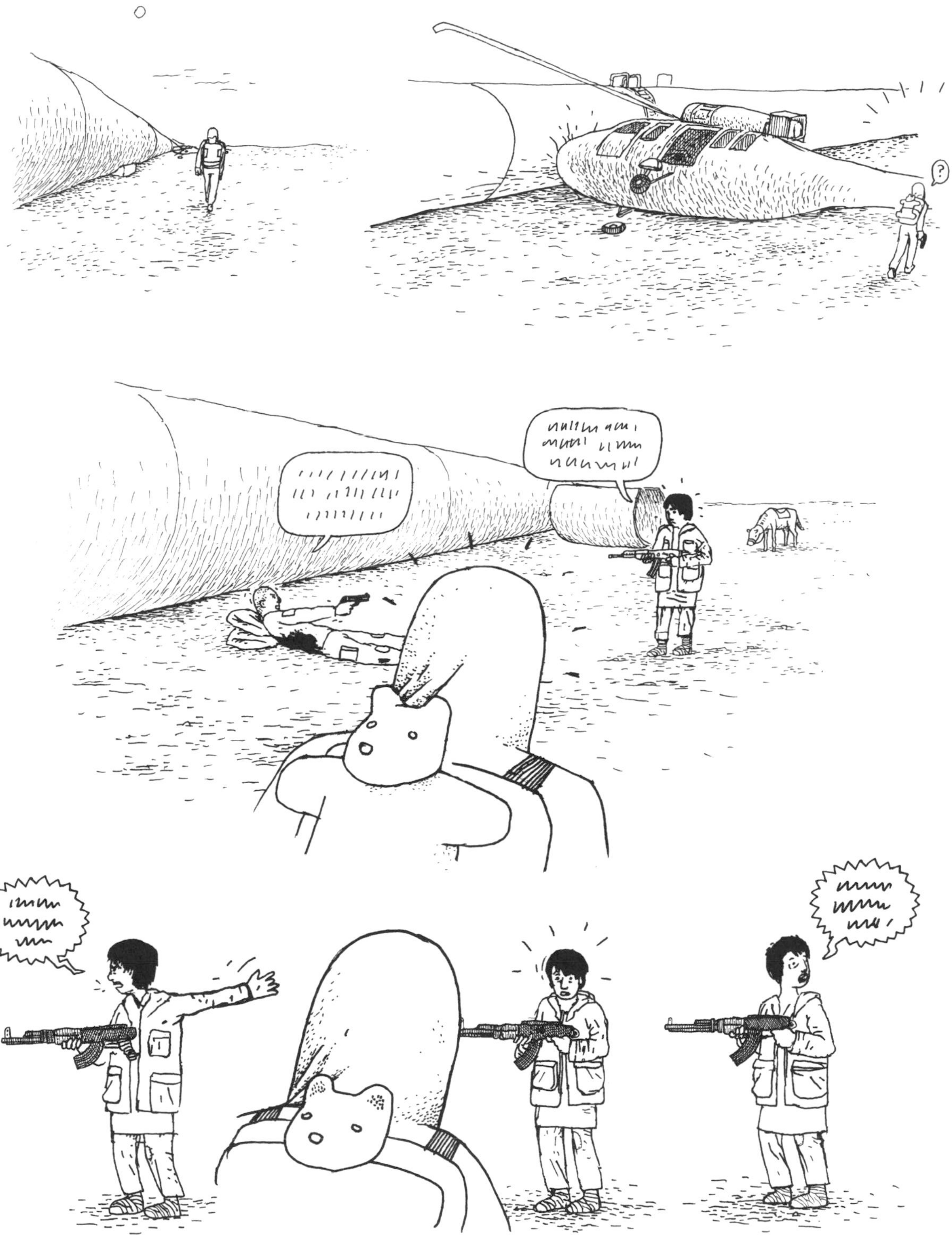
?

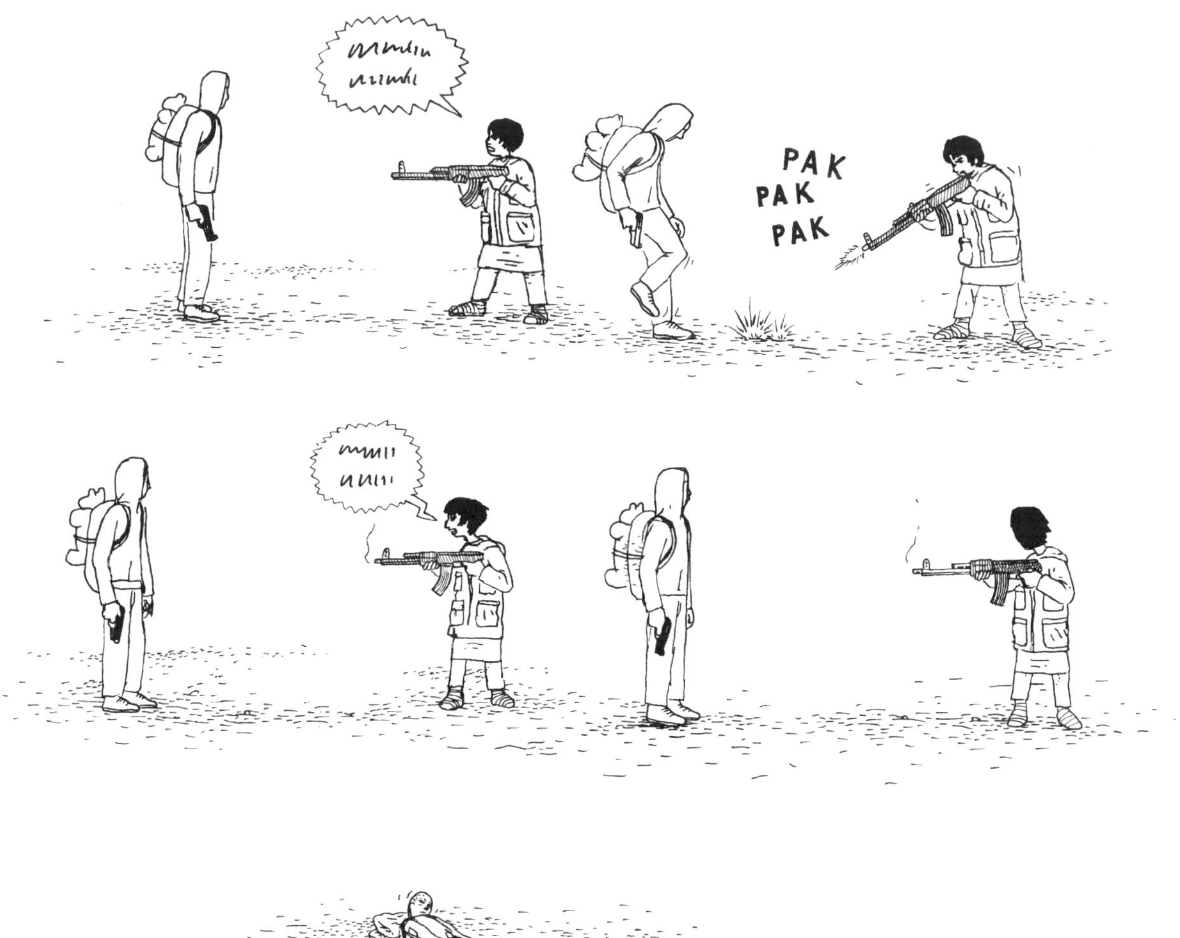
PAK
PAK
PAK

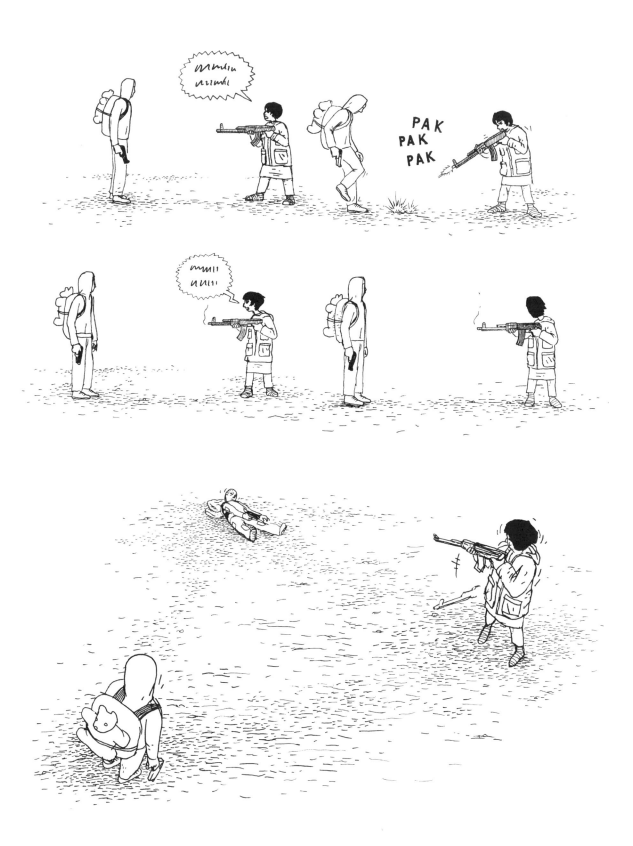

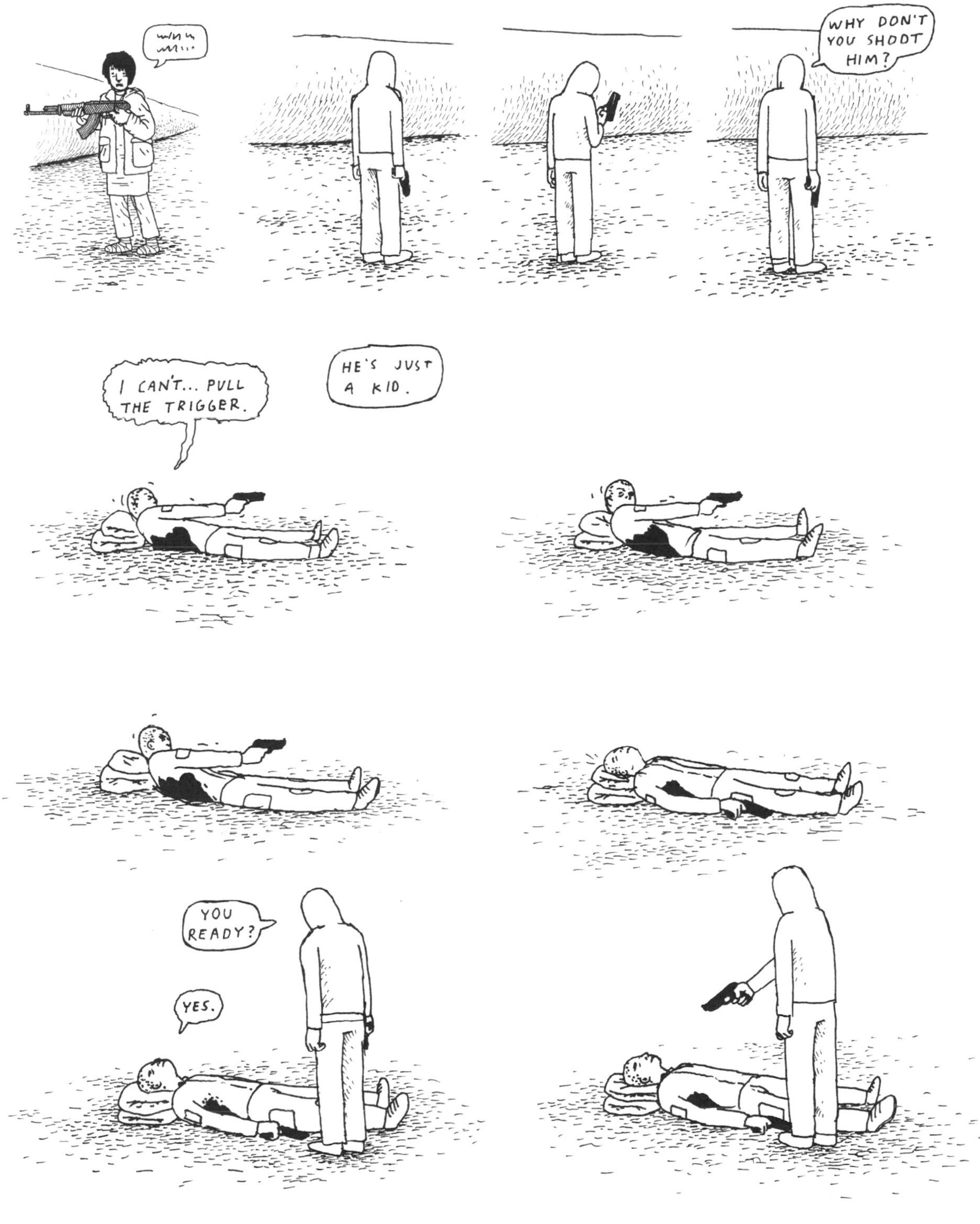
WHY DON'T YOU SHOOT HIM?
I CAN'T... PULL THE TRIGGER.
HE'S JUST A KID.
YOU READY?
YES.

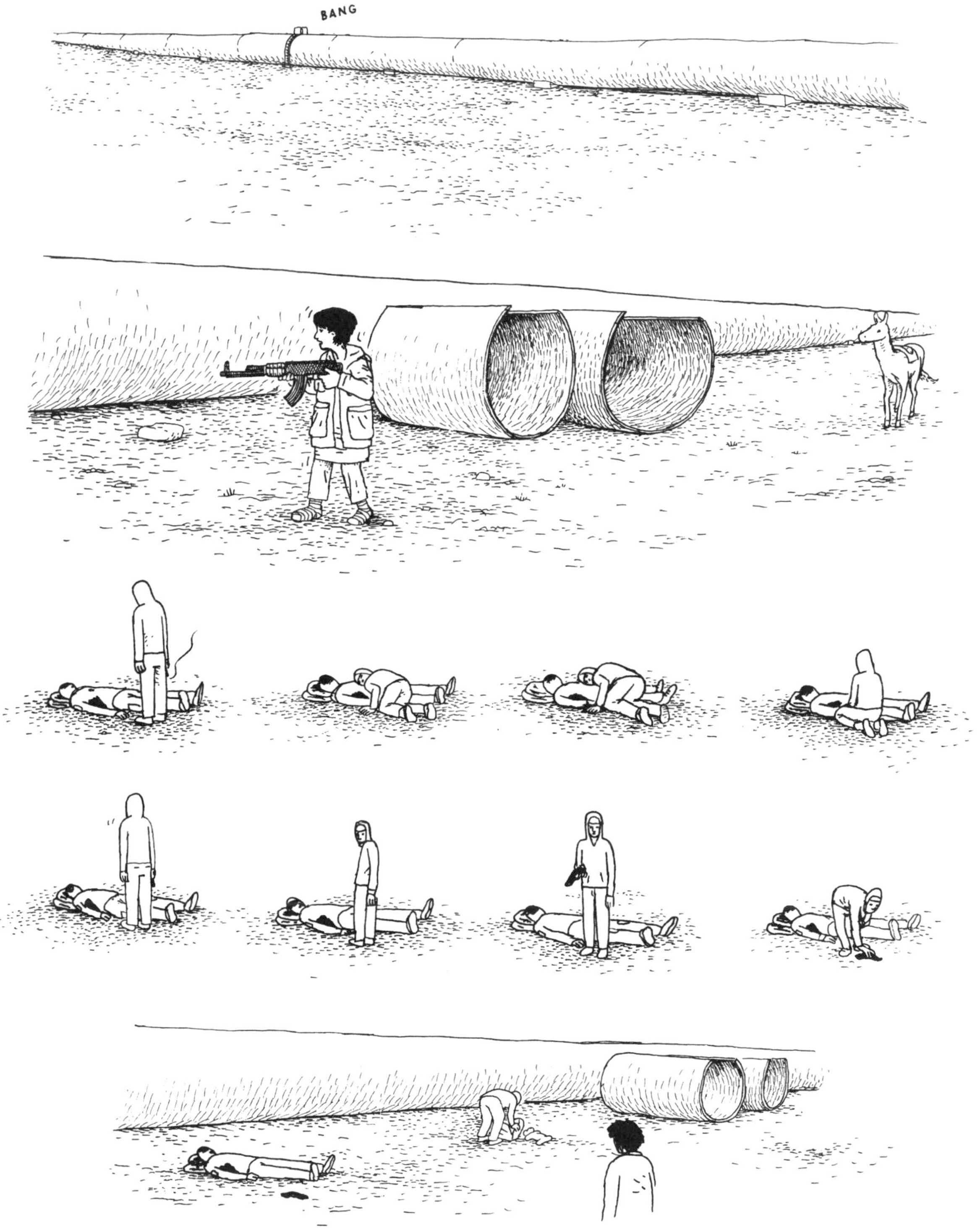
BANG

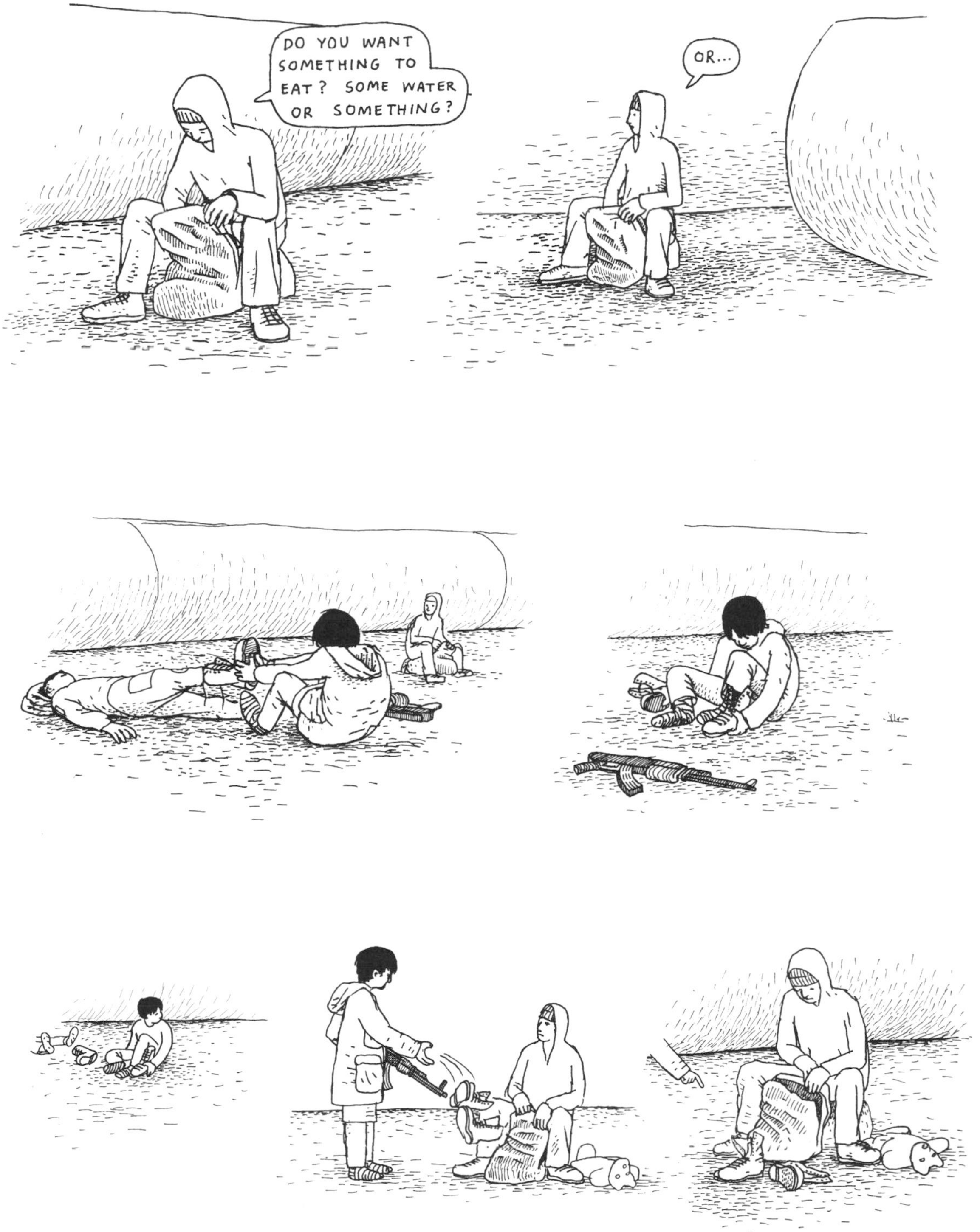
DO YOU WANT SOMETHING TO EAT? SOME WATER OR SOMETHING?
OR...

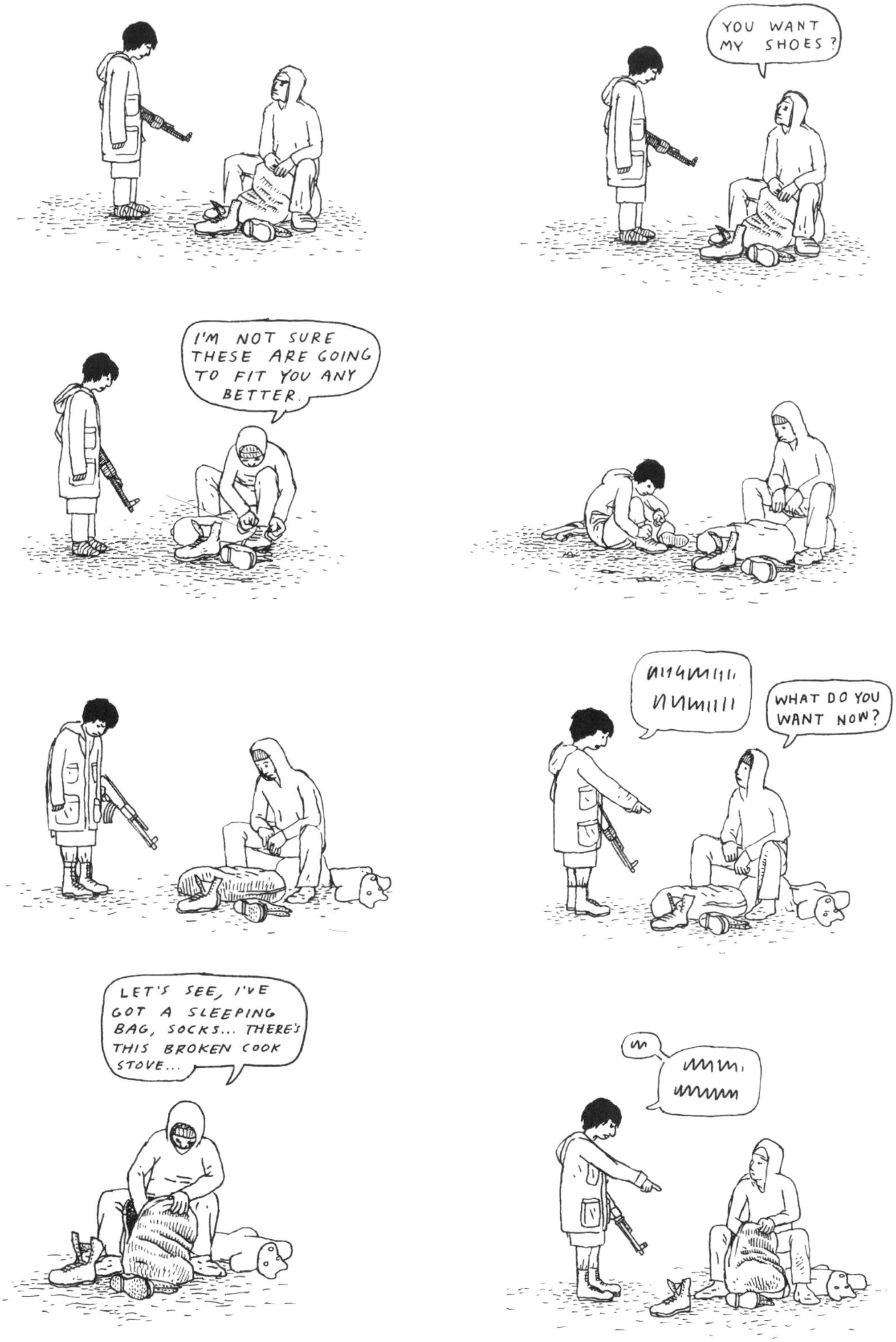
YOU WANT MY SHOES?
I'M NOT SURE THESE ARE GOING TO FIT YOU ANY BETTER.
WHAT DO YOU WANT NOW?
LET'S SEE, I'VE GOT A SLEEPING BAG, SOCKS... THERE'S THIS BROKEN COOK STOVE...

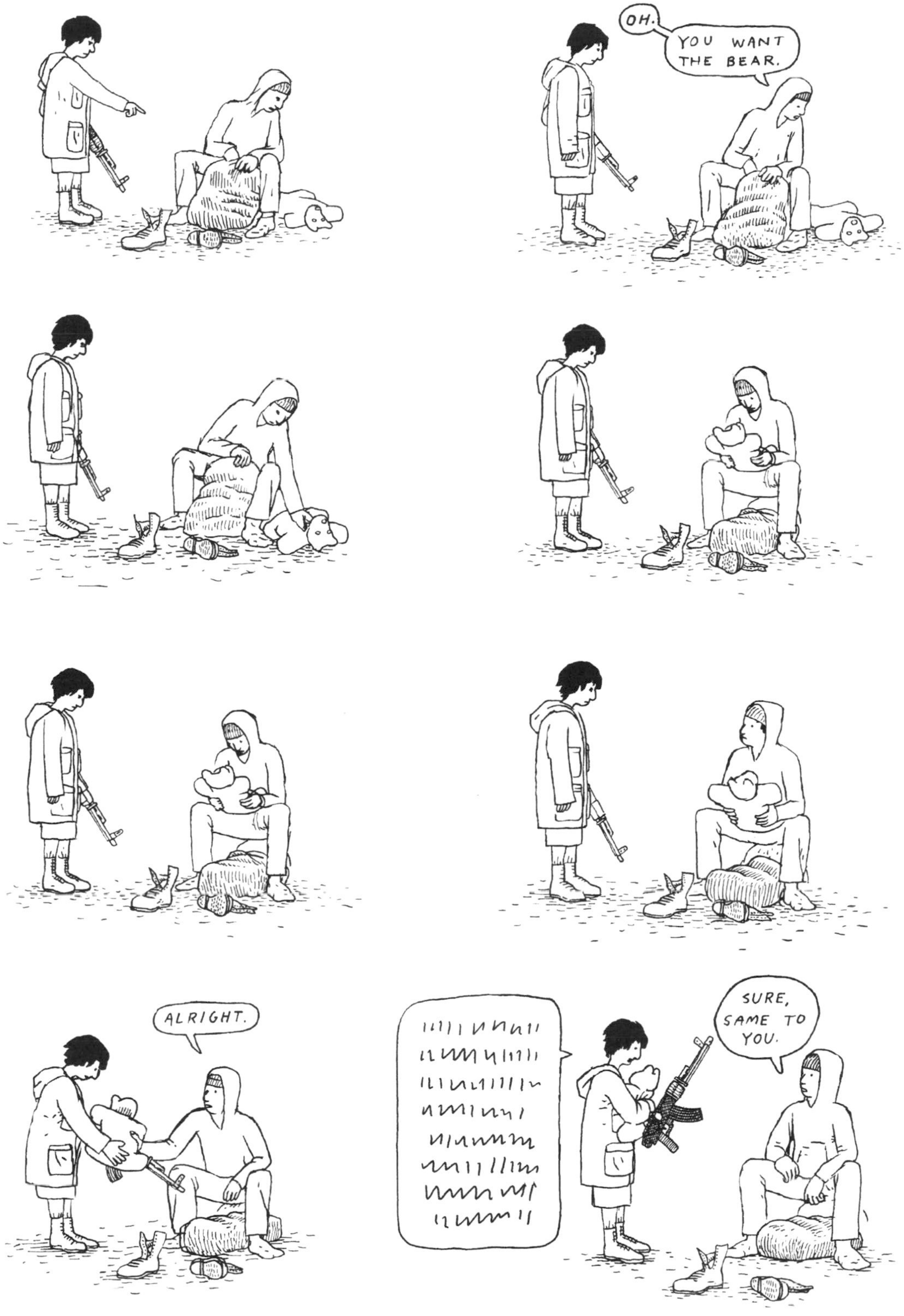

OH.
YOU WANT THE BEAR.
ALRIGHT.
SURE, SAME TO YOU.

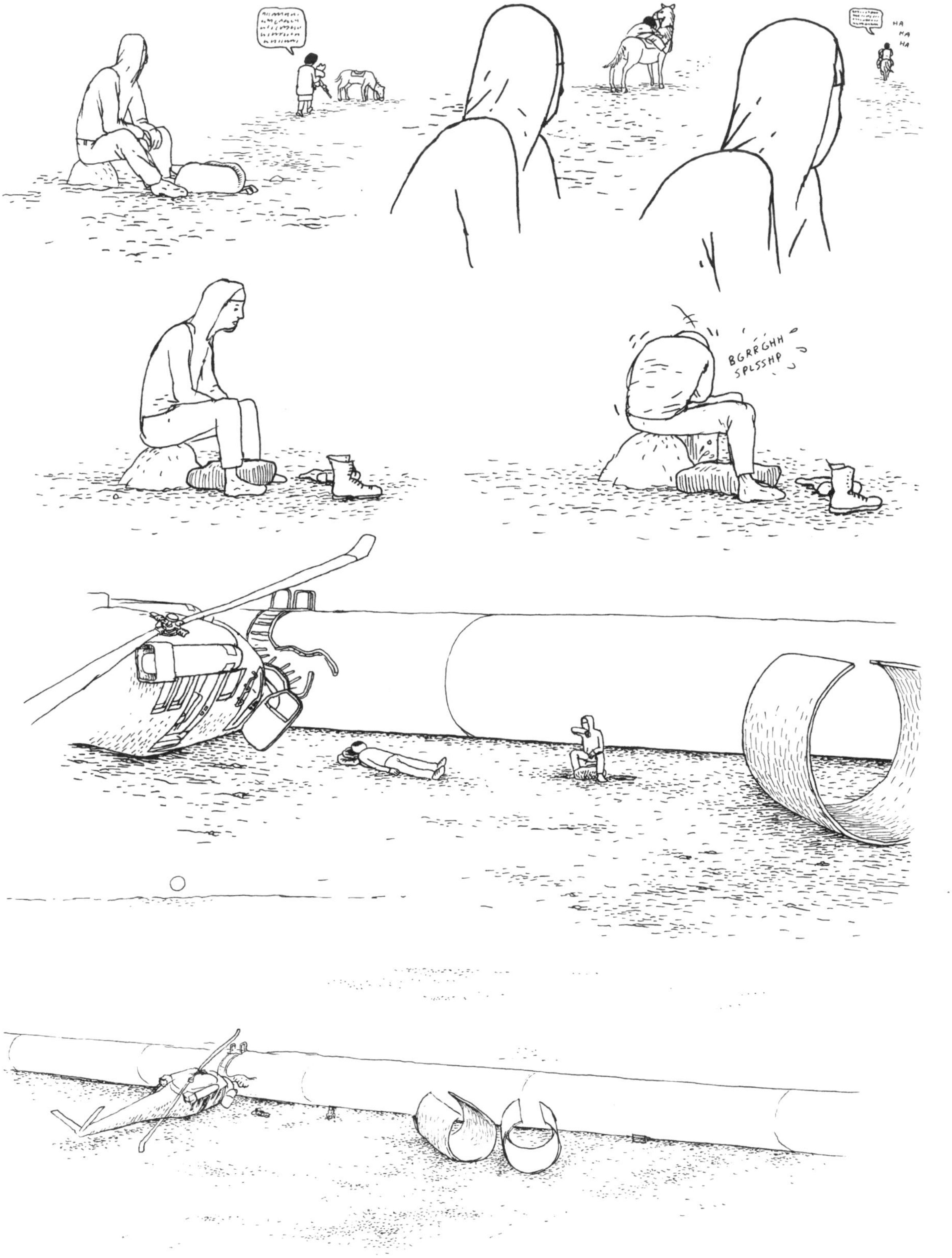
HA
HA
HA
BGRRGHH
SPLSSHP

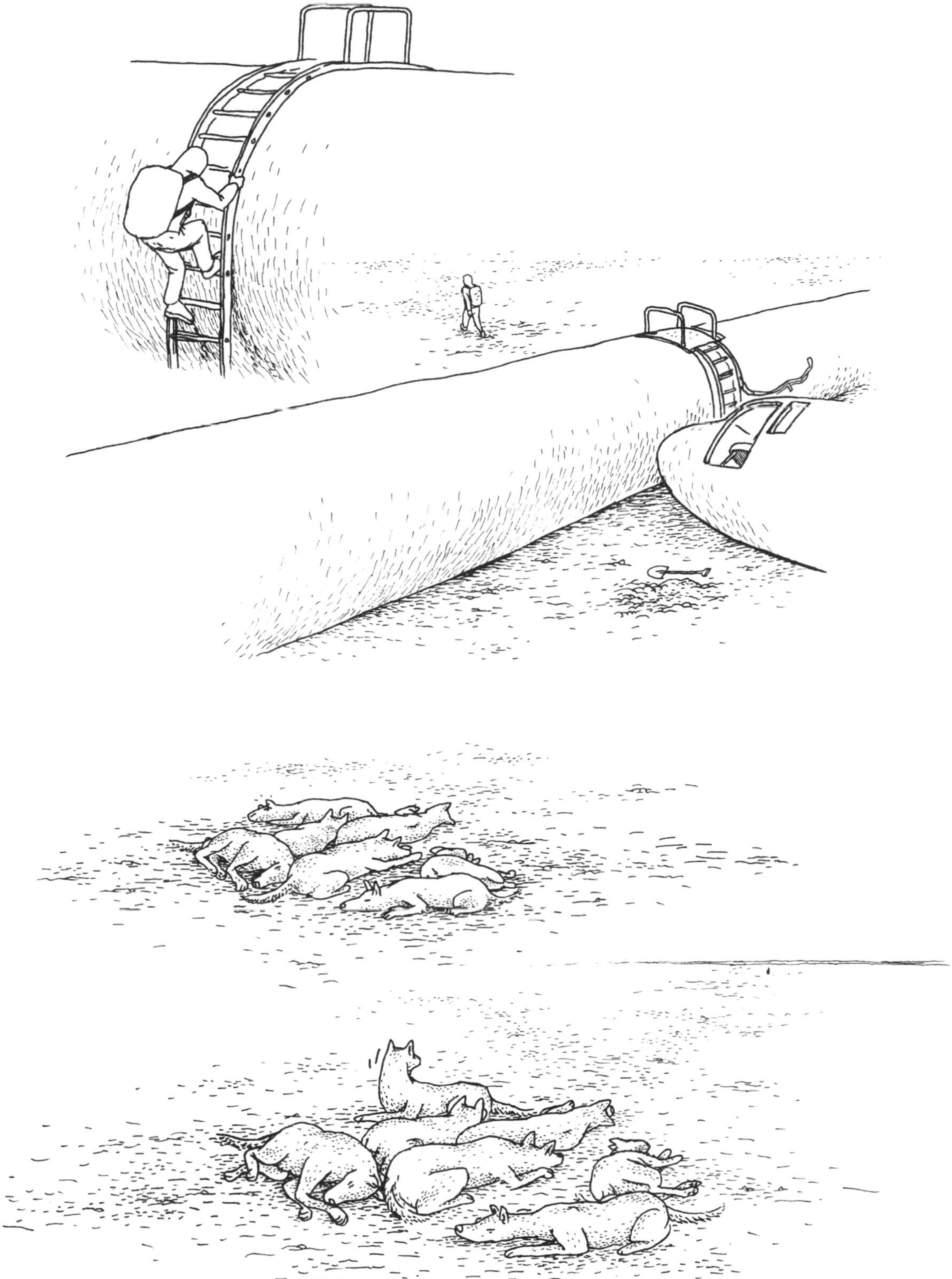

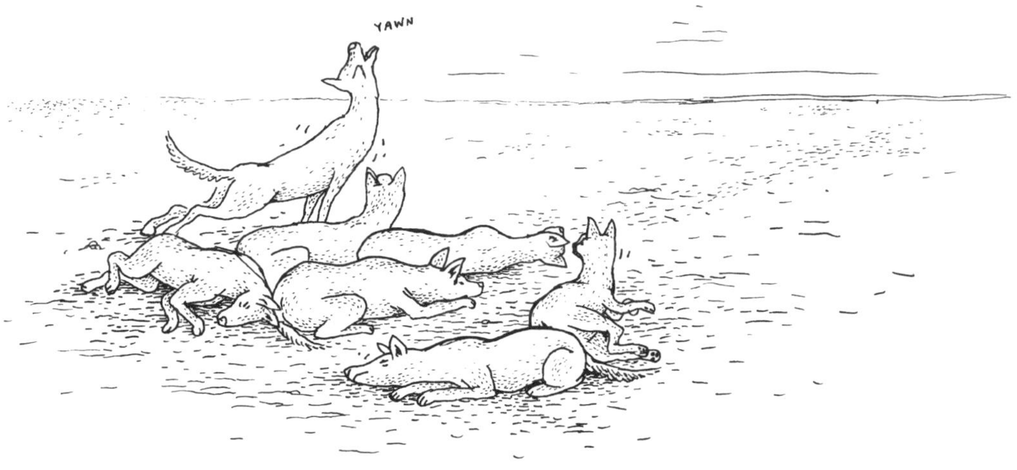
YAWN

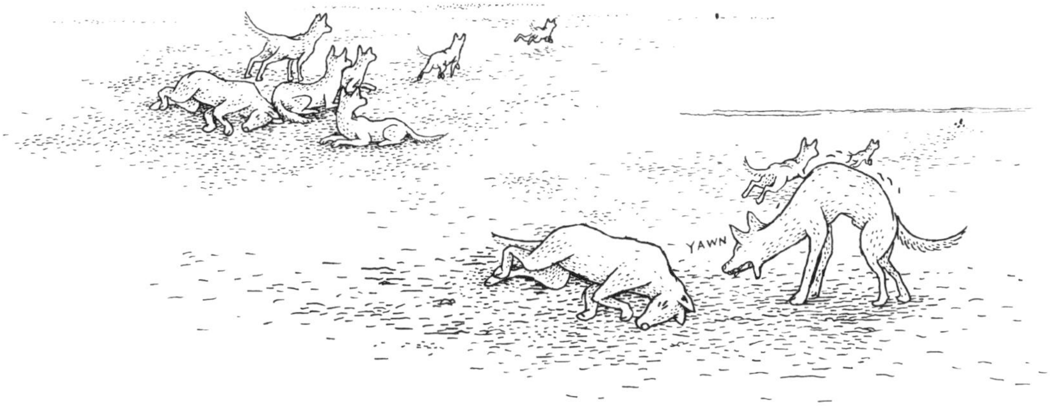
YAWN

THE END

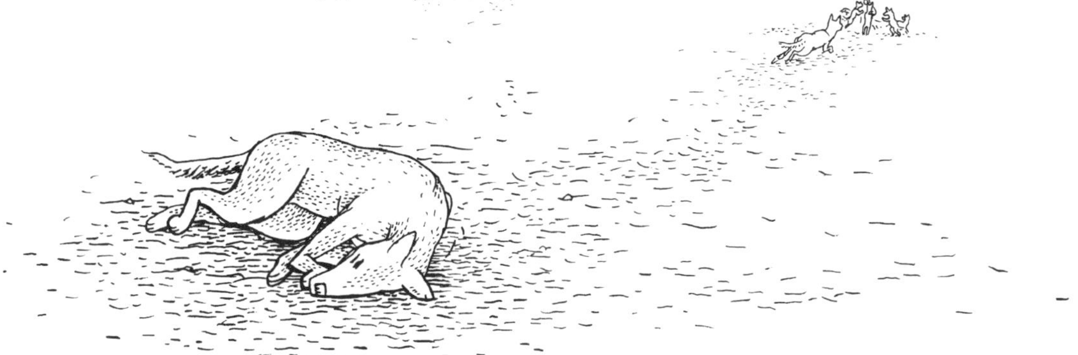

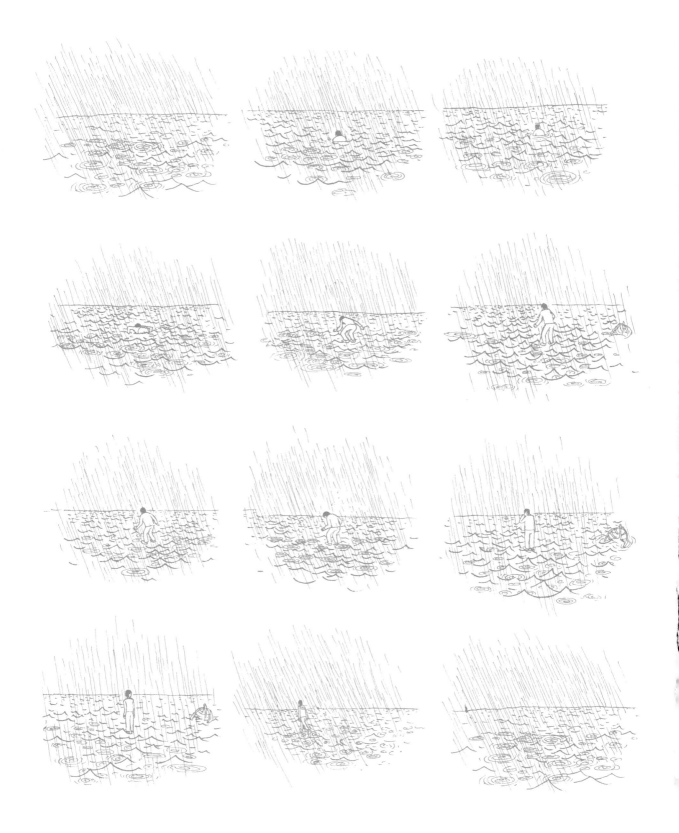

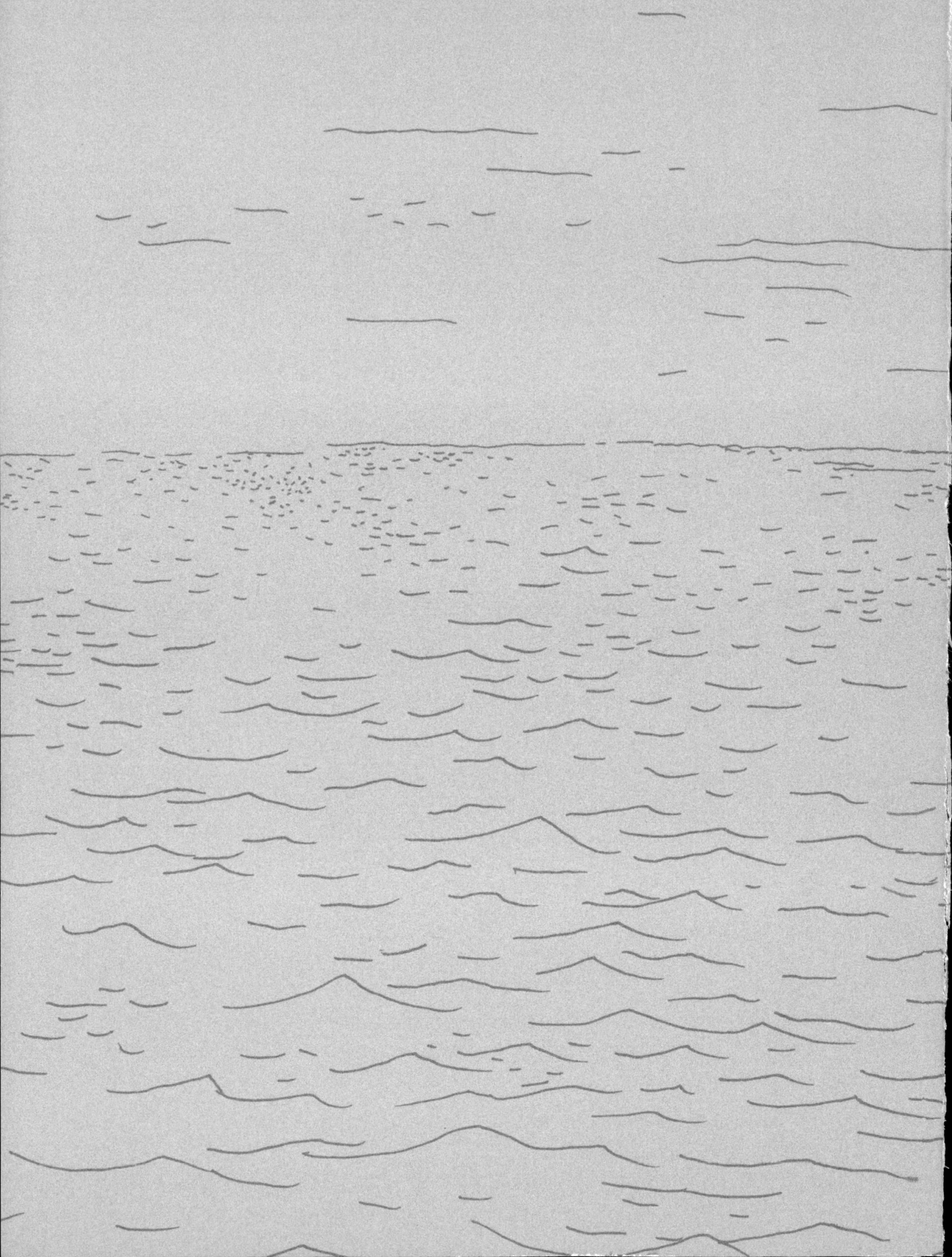